Mallarmé

Mallarmé

by GUY MICHAUD

translated by MARIE COLLINS

and BERTHA HUMEZ

NEW YORK UNIVERSITY PRESS 1965

*The original French Edition of this book appeared under
the title* Mallarmé *and was published by Hatier, Paris.*

CONTENTS

v

74133

CONTENTS

Except as otherwise indicated, page references are to the Bibliothèque de la Pléiade edition of the *Oeuvres complètes* (Complete Works) of Mallarmé.

Throughout the book, whenever a poem of some importance is discussed, there are footnotes referring, by the author's name only, to commentaries upon the poem. A table of these references follows:

Chassé: *les Clefs de Mallarmé* (1954)
Davies: *Les "tombeaux" de Mallarmé* (1950)
Gengoux: *Le symbolisme de Mallarmé* (1950)
Mauron: *Mallarmé l'obscur* (1941)
Mauron II: *Introduction à la psychanalyse de Mallarmé* (1950)
Noulet: *L'oeuvre poétique de Stéphane Mallarmé* (1940)
Noulet II: *Dix poèmes de S. Mallarmé* (1948)
Thibaudet: *La poésie de Stéphane Mallarmé* (1913)
Wais: *Mallarmé, nouvelle édition* (1952)

See Bibliographical Note, pp. 169–172

THE VERSE and prose of Mallarmé quoted in this book have been translated as nearly literally as possible, and with little alteration of word order and punctuation. The translators have felt that the English-speaking reader of an introduction to Mallarmé's intensely individual style would be better served in this way than by any attempt at poetic transmutation or at a polished English smoothness. Mallarmé's intentional ambiguities presented a special problem; we have striven to preserve them rather than to allow the translation to become a simplistic explanation of the complex original.

One word of caution is necessary: Mallarmé often (but not always) uses *idéal* in the philosophical sense of "concerned with ideas, or embodying an archetypal idea." We have rendered it as "ideal." In reading Mallarmé, one does well to bear in mind Wallace Stevens' instructions for reading his "Notes toward a Supreme Fiction":

> You must become an ignorant man again
> And see the sun again with an ignorant eye
> And see it clearly in the idea of it.

Mallarmé

Introduction

IN HIS AUTOBIOGRAPHY, Mallarmé says that since the time of the
Revolution one or another of his ancestors on both sides had
been employed as a civil servant in the Registry. Although he
himself avoided this career (to which, he adds, he was destined
from the cradle), he seems to have inherited the outward appearances of his ancestors. The frail silhouette of the little
English professor at the Collège of Tournon, the shivering
shadow of the lone figure of Valvins, his fragile chin hidden
behind a goatee, the cramped and withdrawn handwriting—
everything about Mallarmé suggested the conscientious, modest
civil servant, inclined by temperament and a natural timidity
toward self-effacement and insignificant positions. Externally,
his life was divided between the continual humiliations of classroom chaos and the domestic worries of a father constantly
preoccupied with "making ends meet." His was the plotless
biography of a man who was above all else, in Claudel's words,
"un homme d'intérieur" a home-loving man.

How could such a drab and banal background bring forth a
body of work that was so novel as to be notorious, and which,
in its originality, aimed at being *unique*? For a long time, Mallarmé's work,

> *Calme bloc ici-bas chu d'un désastre obscur*

> (Calm block fallen here below from an obscure disaster)

presented an unwonted mystery to the reader as well as to the
critic. Albert Thibaudet, one of the most brilliant critics, suc-

ceeded in arousing admiration for Mallarmé's innumerable
facets, but despite his efforts the work remained an unopened
strongbox. Was there a key? After Thibaudet, many took turns
at laborious and brilliant exegeses, all seemingly probable, yet all
devoid of conclusive proof. Then, just when certain critics were
beginning to think that this work, which had provoked so much
sarcasm, might perhaps be indeed a dazzling but empty strongbox, the sudden appearance of the poet's correspondence almost
half a century after his death provided the key that had been
missing. What had heretofore seemed inexplicable now was
made clear: it was the product of a terrible internal drama and
a tenacious will in the service of genius.

The product is no less admirable for that. Many studies have
since accumulated around Mallarmé's work, gradually removing
its enigmatic character and integrating it after a fashion into
the properly "literary" tradition. It is to be hoped that they will
not dim its glory and reduce it to a mere "book among other
books" and "one attempt among others," as Jean Starobinski
fears,[1] but, on the contrary, will help to point out its value as a
unique endeavor and preserve in some way its "absolute difference," in accordance with Mallarmé's wish. In my opinion, to
understand a work does not require dealing with it *along with*
others so as to strip it progressively of its specific traits; rather it
is to be examined *in relationship* with other works and a definition found of its true position in the period from which, to all
appearances, it stems. Only then can it be isolated in the eminent dignity of its solitude.

It is undoubtedly too soon to bring the issue to a close by
publishing a sort of "present state of Mallarmé studies." Even
after Professor Mondor's masterly biography, Jacques Scherer's
scholarly study of Mallarmé's language and syntax, Charles
Mauron's psychoanalytic investigations, and the work on Mallarmé's poetry by E. Noulet, Kurt Wais, Camilla Soula, Antoine
Orliac, Charles Chassé, Jacques Gengoux, Gardner Davies, Guy
Delfel, and others, much remains to be done. The task of the
years to come will be to follow step by step the development
of the total work in its multiple (Mallarmé's) perspectives, to

---

[1] *Les Lettres*, special number, 1948, p. 35.

define precisely the poet's metaphysical and psychological progressions, and to reconstruct, more rigorously than before, the dialectics of an imagination which was the first to attempt a total awareness of its own powers and the lucid construction of a peculiarly poetic language and universe.

My only ambition here is to propose an "introduction to the reading and understanding of Mallarmé": a study that will take special care to fix the landmarks which will situate the diverse investigations already attempted, while at the same time suggesting avenues of future research. Of course I shall occasionally present a personal viewpoint. However, through a method of "open synthesis," I shall endeavor not to confuse the reader or lead him astray, but to keep him within the bounds of the most commonly accepted interpretations.

More in the case of Mallarmé than in any other, the study of a man must be associated today with that of his work. It is true that Mallarmé took great care to discourage future indiscretions with regard to an existence which he himself was the first to label devoid of ancedote. But, apart from ancedotes, the inner biography which governs creation and is inseparable from it cannot be neglected. It has seemed to me that it would constitute the best access to a body of work reputed to be exceedingly difficult. So I have decided to follow the stages of this inner biography as it kept step with the evolution of a creative existence. The poet himself considered the accomplishment of this existence as a rough draft of the Great Work.

NOTE FOR THE THIRD EDITION

Since the first edition of this book, several works important to the understanding of Mallarmé have been published. They have led me to make some clarifications here and there, wherever space would permit. But on the whole the studies seem to confirm rather than question my general interpretations.

Charles Chassé has finally assembled the fruit of long years of research under the title, *Les clefs de Mallarmé* (Mallarmé's Keys). He is convinced that these keys can all be found in the Littré dictionary. The hypothesis is appealing, and it is highly probable that Mallarmé, wanting "to give a purer meaning to the words of the tribe," i.e., to use words in their etymological sense, had recourse to Littré to this end. Nevertheless, I persist in thinking that these "keys" do not by any means open all the doors (Chassé deliberately and arbitrarily excludes "Igitur" and "le Coup de Dés" from his exegesis), especially since the interpretation proposed by these "keys" in no way invalidates other interpretations. Chassé supports his theory with two or three witticisms attributed to Mallarmé by his contemporaries. He can easily be contested by these words of Theodor de Wyzewa, one of those who unquestionably best understood the poet's original intentions: "Each one of his lines was intended to be at once a plastic image, the expression of a thought, the enunciation of a feeling, and a philosophical symbol."

Is believing in these "superimpressions" really to claim, as Chassé accuses me of doing, that "there is no concrete meaning in Mallarmé"?

More decisive, in my opinion, is Jacques Scherer's Le "Livre" de Mallarmé (Mallarmé's "Book"), the publication of an invaluable autograph notebook belonging to Professor Mondor. It bears formal witness to what I have always maintained: that Mallarmé's famous "Book," far from being a myth, was the climax of the entire opus, and gives Wyzewa's theory a "decisive confirmation," as Scherer points out in his remarkable introduction. It also proves that "both the unity and meaning of Mallarmé's creation" can be reconstituted only through an acceptance of the "necessary plurality of meanings" in his poems. For want of space, I have been able to devote only a few sentences (pp. 164–168) to what the "Book" would have been, according to this manuscript. Its publication was a true revelation.

I . Birth of the Poet

1 · The Muse of Impotency

I. THE LAST ROMANTIC

Nothing in his childhood or adolescence seems to have prophesied Stéphane Mallarmé's singular destiny. No glorious father led him at the age of nine through the marvels of Spain, as did Hugo's; nor did he run away at the age of fifteen, as did Rimbaud. There was nothing of the precocious child or the marked genius about him.

He was born in Paris on March 18, 1842. His father, like his grandfather before him, was a civil servant in the Registry. His mother died accidentally upon returning from a trip when he was five, and on this occasion Stéphane threw himself on the floor and tore his hair. Was this really only play-acting—feigning a sorrow which he was disturbed not to feel, as he later asserted to Henri de Régnier? Or does such an attitude not indicate a mixture of sham and unconscious bewilderment, the expression of a shock experienced in the very depths of his being? After all, the grandmother who took charge of his education, while later deploring the fact that he was so unstudious, did delight in the goodness of his heart.

Upon his father's rather early remarriage, Stéphane was sent at the age of ten to a boarding school in Auteuil. It was a Catholic school, attended by "society" children, and the boy felt ill at ease. Try as he might to escape the contemptuous teasing and blows of his classmates by exchanging his commoner's name for a more flattering one and claiming to be the "Count of Boulainvilliers," this first contact with society gave

7

him an inferiority complex. Its first effects showed shortly thereafter: He withdrew into himself, his teachers complained that
he was "vain and rebellious," and his grandmother noted sadly
that his character was becoming touchy and aggressive. Could
his timidity be developing into revolt?

More probably, Stéphane Mallarmé of the "Lamartinian soul,"
as he later described himself at this stage, was already seeking
escape from a hostile world in dream. The dream was peopled
with cherubim and mystical visions, as a narrative written when
he was eleven testifies. "L'Ange gardien" (The Guardian
Angel) undoubtedly reveals more than just a simple expression
of pious imagery:

> Oh! pourquoi, bon ange, cachez-vous votre tête sous votre blanche
> aile et pourquoi pleurez-vous ainsi? Ah! je le comprends, c'est que
> l'avenir du jeune homme ne sera pas comme il le pense et qu'il doit
> vous coûter bien des chagrins. Et lorsqu'il est lancé au milieu du
> monde, seul vous veillez autour de lui, seul vous ne le quittez jamais,
> vous remplacez une mère qu'il a peut-être perdue.

(Oh! Why do you hide your head under your white wing and
why do you cry so, good angel? Ah! I understand, it is because the
young man's future will not be what he expects, and he will cause
you much pain. And when he is flung into the world, only you will
watch over him, only you will never leave him, you will replace a
mother whom perhaps he has lost.)

In the change of direction of a single sentence, we perceive the
echo of a still unreasoned fear, mingled with nostalgia for the
maternal tenderness which he had not known and an aspiration
toward a purer world.

At fifteen, another trial awaited him: the death of his younger
sister, Maria, confidante of his childhood joys. "Ce que disaient
les Trois Cigognes" (What the Three Storks Said), a "narrative on a free subject" written in school in the second or third
grade and published by Professor Mondor in his *Mallarmé plus
intime* (A More Intimate Mallarmé), is indubitably a transposition into poetry of the emotional disorder which mourning inspired in his adolescent soul. Nick Parritt, a poor wood-
cutter, alone in his cabin with his cat by the dying fire, dreams
of his dead young daughter with such intensity that, led by a
seraph, she leaves her grave and pays her father a visit. Who can

fail to see here the future poet of "les Fenêtres" (Windows) and "les Fleurs" (Flowers)—shivering, obsessed by winter, attempting to conjure away the powers of death by surrendering to a mystical dream in a white décor of snow, moon, lilies, and roses?

Until he was eighteen, Stéphane's religious education, coupled with his secret suffering, only heightened the natural tendencies of a passive and dreamy temperament. The only adolescent poems that Mallarmé did not destroy, the "Cantate pour la Première Communion" (Cantata for the First Communion) of 1858 and the diptych: "Sa fosse est creusée! . . . Sa fosse est fermée" (Her Grave Is Dug! . . . Her Grave Is Closed) of 1859 indicate the same romantic insistence; he describes angels dressed in azure gowns and uses the same antithesis between images of death or the coffin and the ascent to heaven of young virgins surrounded by lilies. His childhood admiration for Béranger merely gave way at this time to the cult of Victor Hugo, whose glory at that moment in the eyes of schoolboys was enhanced by the enchantment of exile. Young Stéphane celebrated this cult secretly in many notebooks of verse which, as he later related, were confiscated one after the other.

This apparently uneventful schoolboy adolescence came to a close, its solitude scarcely attenuated by a few comradeships or budding friendships with Emmanuel Bailly and perhaps with another young poet four years his senior, Eugène Lefébure. But at least a vocation had been asserted in this withdrawn and profoundly wounded soul, one far removed from the calling that he was expected to inherit from his ancestors.

II. THE FIRST DECADENT

However, as soon as his baccalaureate was over, he took a supernumerary's job with the Registry at Sens. Scribbling away on official documents was not exactly to his taste. Liberated from the constraint of school, he probably preferred to stroll, gazing in bookshop windows looking for some new poet, or perhaps give free rein to certain demands of his temperament which had hitherto remained dormant. But why was the venerable Madame Desmoulins concerned about her grandson's relaxations when he never had a cent in his pockets, as he confided to his friend Cazalis? In that calm county, the "youthful priapism" of which he accused himself later was probably limited to a few inconsequential adventures, only distantly reminiscent of the bohemian life his Romantic masters inspired in his dreams.

The year 1861 did bring about fortuitously his first great literary encounter. The second edition of *Les Fleurs du Mal* (Flowers of Evil) had just come out. Everything about Baudelaire was calculated to attract him. Novelty, first of all—that taste of forbidden fruit savored by every young man of nineteen upon leaving the restrictions of the classroom. And then the Baudelairean landscape—its sky livid with boredom, its setting sun, its "angels white as Hosts singing their ecstasy and playing harps that resemble their wings," as he noted later—was very much in tune with Mallarmé's dreamy, melancholy, and mystical temperament. Mallarmé defined this landscape in one of his first prose poems inspired by Baudelaire, "Plainte d'Automne" (Autumn Complaint). Here the red and yellow beams of the waning sun summon up in his mind the dying poetry of the Latin decadence and "tout ce qui se résume en ce mot: chute" (all that the word "fall" summarizes).

Led by his new master in poetry, Mallarmé would slowly rid himself of his youthful admiration for Victor Hugo and Romantic lyricism. He learned the value of density and concision. He learned, too, not to recoil before the brutal expression of sensuality, as can be seen in "Galanterie macabre" (Macabre Gallantry) and "l'Enfant prodigue" (The Prodigal Son), both written during this period. The imitation in these poems seems at times to become mere pastiche. Nonetheless, a new aspect of Mallarmé is to be discovered here: an almost morbid eroticism, from which the poet more than once demands an escape from his anguish. But even more, these poems, which contrast dream to boredom, Infinity to the Abyss, reveal that Mallarmé, thanks to Baudelaire, was beginning to become aware of the "double postulation" which tore him too: the obsession with death and the thirst for the ideal. Yet he did not see himself for very long in this Baudelairean vocabulary. The discovery of Baudelaire was still only an approximation for Mallarmé, in a language which was not yet his own and which did not correspond to his inner self—his true "moi."

At this point (October, 1861) a young professor, Emmanuel des Essarts, arrived at the Lycée of Sens. He claimed to be a figure in the Parisian literary world. The older and the younger man soon became friends. It was a brotherly friendship to which Mallarmé gave himself completely. A new world was opening to him. For the first time, he could confide his poetic ambitions to someone capable of understanding them. Thanks to Emmanuel, the young poet would soon be able to make his entrance into literature. Des Essarts also brought with him the fresh air of the capital. It was a time when new stars were rising on the poetic horizon. Leconte de Lisle's glory was supplanting Hugo's, the younger generation was manifesting its excitement in the pages of *l'Artiste* or the *Revue fantaisiste,* just founded by an ambitious and resourceful eighteen-year-old, Catulle Mendès, with Louis Bouilhet, Glatigny, Villiers de l'Isle-Adam, and other friends of des Essarts. Following the example of Gautier's and Baudelaire's protests against the superabundant lyricism and subjective outpourings of the Romantic soul, they began to proclaim the superiority of impersonal poetry with clear contours and impeccable plasticity. The expectation of something about to happen was in the air—a group, a school, lacking only a leader, who could well be Leconte de Lisle unless the honor fell to Théodore de Banville, another "elder" of forty whose optimistic fantasy and growing glory were undeniably attractive.

Mallarmé may have owed this second discovery to des Essarts. It is a fact that the influence of the Banville of *Odes funambulesques* (Grotesque Odes), counterbalancing that of Baudelaire, gave rise in him to new images and themes. The best example of this is the charming piece in a very eighteenth-century tone: "Petite laveuse blonde" (Little Blond Laundress). A pleasant dream has turned her into both a fauness and a marquise waving a *fan* bathed with *foam* amidst *roses* and *gladioli* made of the finest *gold.* How remarkable to find already in their pure state, mounted in convoluted arabesques, a certain number of the images which haunted Mallarmé's poetry up to the end! Here we are in the presence of the faun's awakening. In this brief and happy period when Mallarmé was discovering both

poetry and friendship, the faun dictated to him pieces of a
veiled and discreet eroticism. It is possible to determine this by
examining "Placet" (which, reworked, later became "Placet
futile"). The poet derives amusement from depicting himself
here as if painted by Boucher on a pink fan, "a flute in his
hands," i.e., in the eventual attitude of the faun.

Mallarmé made his début in letters with this graceful if inconsequential sonnet. Des Essarts' efforts, albeit selfish, helped
the piece to appear at the beginning of 1862 in a modest and
short-lived review, le Papillon (The Butterfly). Actually, Mallarmé had already appeared in it with a sincerely complimentary
review of Poésies parisiennes, which his friend had just published. Apropos of these poems he had written this revealing
sentence: "An ideal which does not exist at all through its own
dream and which is the lyricism of reality, such is the intention
of Poésies parisiennes." As Georges Poulet has ingeniously
pointed out, turn the formula around and Mallarmé's secret is
compressed in one line: "An ideal which exists through its own
dream and is not the lyricism of reality." If, for the moment,
Mallarmé had not yet rejected all lyricism, his poetry had already broken with reality and, freed from any attachment to it,
demanded its justification only from the dream; just as the beggars of the blue (l'azur) in "le Guignon" (Evil Genie) biting
"au citron d'or de l'idéal amer" (into the golden lemon of the
bitter ideal) or "le Sonneur" (Bellringer) pulling "le câble à
sonner l'Idéal" (the rope to ring the Ideal).

III. IMPOTENCY AND POETIC VOCATION

These two poems, which appeared in turn in March of 1862
in l'Artiste, have nothing in common with "Placet." It could
be said that with "Haine du pauvre" (Hate of the Poor Man;
later "Aumône" [Alms]) they still show development in the
Baudelairean vein, were it not for the fact that "le Guignon,"
though its title is certainly Baudelairean, has some obvious
echoes of Théophile Gautier. But what is significant here is that
the meeting of these two masters led Mallarmé to become conscious of his vocation and his condition as a poet. He heard a
call, a "voice," and at once this voice seemed to him a distant,
infinitely distant, faint chiming, sent into an ideal and inac-

cessible heaven. The decadent Romanticism here must be acknowledged: invocations to Satan, the descriptions of the
mountebanks "assoiffés de grand" (thirsting for grandeur) who
defy Hell even as they jump under the whip of the Guignon,
or even the somewhat literary despair which leads them, as
it leads the bellringer, to hang themselves to escape their pain.
Nevertheless, in both these poems, the problem is posed: How
can the poet, a new Hamlet,[1] reconcile an imperious vocation
with the inaccessibility of his ideal? The tense, anguished conflict which an entire life would not suffice to resolve was being
born in Mallarmé.

With the advent of spring he was possessed by the "curious
sterility" and "impotency" which he confessed three months
later in a letter to his new friend, Cazalis. The feeling never left
him. It is easy to explain this impotency by recalling the exces-
sive demands the poet made on his art. From this moment on,
we find Mallarmé declaring that he "often spent three days in
balancing the parts [of a sonnet] in advance so that the whole
might be harmonious and approach the Beautiful." In reality,
impotency was a torture for him because it lived in him like a
familiar demon, ingrained in his very character, a character
which he had only just discovered. There were really at least
two contradictory beings in Mallarmé: one warm, passionate,
overflowing with enthusiasm and lyricism; the other cold, self-
doubting, withdrawn, exacting, avid too, but of purity and the
absolute. And how could the first, in spite of all its ardor, attain
that ideal sky whose purity was so jealously defended by the
other?

At the end of "three months of impotency," Mallarmé could
find only one way of exorcising the monster: execrating it in
verse. So he wrote "Renouveau" (Renewal), a poem in which
this time the sound and movement are unmistakably his own,
in spite of persistently Baudelairean accents. After lucid winter,
the season of work, comes sickly spring, the season of impotency, i.e., of waiting, vague and lazy reverie, then lassitude,

---

[1] Hamlet's name, which haunted Mallarmé all his life, figures in the
first version of "le Guignon" as well as in his first letter to Cazalis, where
he characterizes himself as "a ridiculous Hamlet who cannot recognize his
collapse."

and finally collapse. Why this almost despairing tone? For the first time, Mallarmé realized that his dream, that "vague and beautiful dream" *had nothing to do with his true ideal.* He was faced, on the one hand, with the facile musings of an adolescent, yielding complacently to the demands of his temperament and abandoning himself to sweet, perfumed visions; and, on the other, with the demands of his character, which even as it *"dug its dream's grave"* craved to be *lifted* toward the inaccessible Blue.

IV. MYSTERY, THE KEY TO POETRY

Having warded off the first crisis through poetry, Mallarmé seems to have recovered his equilibrium. Summer was approaching. Sometimes the young provincial would join some of his new friends in the forest of Fontainebleau, halfway between Sens and Paris. "Vagabond races from rock to rock" and "sun in the eyes and in the heart" marked these excursions with Cazalis, des Essarts, and the very popular poetess-pianist, Nina de Villard. It was perhaps on returning to Sens after such a day that he described the "drunken fauns in the moss" in the light poem, "Soleil d'Hiver" (Winter Sun), published shortly thereafter by the obscure *Journal des Baigneurs* (Bathers' Newspaper) in Dieppe. Sometimes too, he would wait at the entrance to the lycée for a young German governess whose blond hair and melancholy glance had struck him. To capture the heart of this "little bird," as he wrote to Cazalis, he would "set up skylarks' mirrors in the field of gallantry." But he was quickly caught in the game and was soon sending Marie Gerhard impassioned letters which never remained long unanswered.

In the midst of his amorous pursuits, Mallarmé, now freed of his obsessive anxiety, returned to his poetry. In an epigrammatic sonnet addressed to des Essarts, "Contre un Poète parisien" (Against a Parisian Poet), he evoked in turn Dante, draped in a shroud; Anacreon, nude and kissing a cluster of grapes; and the great bohemians, mad for the blue. Was he perhaps aware, then, that he bore within himself not only two, but three poets: the "Saturnian" who imitated Baudelaire, the faun, and the lover of the ideal?

In any case, he was now preoccupied with defining, once and

for all, *his* poetry—or at least the idea he had of poetry. Diverse
influences had been preparing him in this direction for a year.
In addition to Baudelaire, to whom he owed his taste for
density, his cult of poetic creation, and his conviction of its
religious and quasi-mystical value, there was Banville, who made
him conscious of his own penchant for preciousness. There was
Théophile Gautier's obsession with the ideal and the blue;
and most of all there was Edgar Allan Poe, whom he had been
avidly reading for several months. Poe, whose poems Mallarmé
was even planning to translate into French, taught him the importance of care and calculation in poetry. There was also
Villiers de l'Isle-Adam's "Isis," just read by Mallarmé, in which
there was a purity-thirsty heroine enveloped in haughty mystery.
Undoubtedly he had also heard the echoes of the *Tannhaüser*
battle in Paris the year before, if only through Baudelaire's
articles, which had recently appeared in the *Revue Europé-
enne*. It must have inspired him to reflect upon the ties between poetry and music. Imbued with all these influences and
stimulated by the crisis he had just passed through, Mallarmé,
in a single burst, composed a manifesto in a tone of hitherto
unknown authority. The piece was not mentioned again until
a modern critic, Madame E. Noulet, exhumed it from the issue
of *l'Artiste* in which it was published on September 15, 1862.

And yet the article—"Hérésie artistique: l'Art pour tous"
(Artistic Heresy: Art for All)—is of major importance, because it contains something approximating a key to his entire
work. Mallarmé goes further than the theoreticians of Art for
Art's Sake and takes his point of departure from a very ingenious idea which he develops with rigorous logic: "Everything
sacred which wishes to remain so is enveloped in mystery." Art,
like religion, is sacred. Certain arts, such as music, use difficult
signs which make them mysterious for the layman. Music has
its secrets; *why then should not poetry?* The public should be
cured of the notion that authentic poetry can be read by anyone
at all, without preparation or culture, like the verse of a M.
Legouvé or the prose of a Viscount du Terrail. It is indispensable to restore dignity to poetry and preserve it from all easy,
vague, and stupid admiration. Thus *the access to it must be
made difficult*. There are precedents for this: "Oh! golden clasps

of old missals! Oh! inviolate hieroglyphics of papyrus rolls!"
Why not restore to poetry the sacred character which once, for
the Middle Ages as well as for certain ancient peoples, restricted
its access to the initiated?

Hence a *closed* poetry, its meaning at first hidden from the
reader, is required. Yet, if Mallarmé was henceforth oriented
toward hermeticism, he was not driven to writing differently
from others by a feeling of vanity, nor, as would be claimed,
by some pleasure derived from gratuitous mystification. It was
because he already had a very lofty notion of his art and was
determined to give it back its religious and sacred nature; because, too, he was aware that this concept of poetry precisely
satisfied the demands of his own character, in which poetic instinct, haughty reserve, and a thirst for purity were combined
and often in conflict.

At twenty, Mallarmé had found the principle of his poetry.
It remained for him to discover how to achieve it.

2 · The Studied Esthetic

> The *effect produced*, that is what I am looking for.
>
> LETTER TO CAZALIS

1. LONDON. "LES FENÊTRES," "APPARITION"

Despite the exaltation of discovery, the summer of 1862 did not bring the amorous young poet the joys he anticipated. Rainy, foreboding weather prevented him from leaving on holiday as he had hoped. His father was ill and his wallet was empty. He wrote to Cazalis: "To think that happiness is sometimes contained in the glimmer of two coins!" Of course, his love was crowned with success; he announced that he belonged to Marie "head and heart" and was incapable of thinking of anything else but her; but family surveillance had to be foiled or provincial prejudices braved, and a few days' escape to Fontainebleau hardly satisfied the ardor of the new lovers.

Happily, Stéphane had projects. In order to "read Poe better" he had been studying English fervidly for several months. He also had in mind a trip to England to perfect his knowledge of the language, so that he could obtain a teaching position which would assure him of independence. So in November he embarked for London with Marie Gerhard, to the great despair of his grandmother, who later recalled "arming him before his departure with her most pressing recommendations for his good behavior, and with several recommendations to all the honorable classes of British society."

It soon became clear that the sojourn in London was not very propitious for poetry. The difficulties caused by their precarious lodging, the London fog, a persistent cough, and material worries were all handicaps to both love and inspiration.

17

That year abroad was a series of separations and reconciliations
until, after lengthy and tortured hesitations, Stéphane decided
to marry Marie, not for himself but "only for her." Thus, according to Stéphane, it would be a marriage of reason; and yet
"she had a look of her own which had once and for all penetrated my soul."

Upon the entreaties of his new friend Cazalis, he dreamed of
going to Switzerland with her. "There is so much blue over
there, besides the sky—and Marie's eyes would follow me
there, . . ." to say nothing of the "virginal glaciers and the snow
which is a flower, like lilies." Mallarmé's marriage had not quite
brought his dream down to earth. Although these difficult
months caused him to shed many illusions, he was nonetheless
determined to safeguard his dream from all the impurities of
life.

A modern poet has carried his stupidity so far as to regret that
"Action is not the sister of the Dream." . . . If the dream were
thus deflowered and abased, where then could we flee, we the un-
fortunates whom the earth disgusts and who have no refuge but the
Dream? Oh, my Henri, quench your thirst with the Ideal. The
happiness of this world is vile . . . only very calloused hands can
harvest it. To say: "I am happy" is to say: "I am a coward" and
more often "I am a fool." For either one must fail to see the sky
of the Ideal above the ceiling of happiness, or one must deliberately
close one's eyes. I have made a little poem of these ideas: "les
Fenêtres" [windows], which I am sending you with another,
"l'Assaut" [Assault], vague and frail as a reverie (to Cazalis, June
3, 1863).

In this commentary, Mallarmé reveals the meaning of "les
Fenêtres," a poem born of the haze and cares of the London
winter. More and more there are two worlds for him: the one
we live in and the ideal world. To be content with the former
and its illusion of happiness is cowardice. To flee it by any route
is thus an act of courage. And to want to flee is to open one's
eyes, to be capable of seeing "the sky of the Ideal above the
ceiling of happiness." This simple sentence also contains several
very important indications. It reveals for the first time the simultaneous presence of a double obsession in Mallarmé: that of a
room and a ceiling which closes it down (colloquial transposition of Baudelaire's prison and its "cover"), and that of the

sky which is beyond. Thanks to the double metaphor ceiling/ happiness, sky/ideal, it reveals too the poet's new consciousness of an *analogy* in structure between the external and internal worlds, an analogy which will lead him gradually toward symbolism. For the moment the poem is still composed according to the classic bipartite formula: a comparison between a dying man endeavoring to escape the horror of the sad hospital through visions of the setting sun, and the poet fleeing human stupidity into the "anterior sky where Beauty flourishes." But the two levels are already incessantly confused: the bored crucifix, the mouth "of a voracious azure blue," the windowpane identified with art or mysticism, the dream worn as a diadem— all are metaphorical expressions affirming by their mere presence the unifying virtue of the poetic act. At the heart of all these expressions appears an image already heavy with symbolic potentialities. The window, and more precisely the square frame, the pane of glass, the crystal, promise of escape, would assure the poet's passage from the real to the ideal world, not because he crosses over this border but because, thanks to the windowpane which is also a *mirror,* the poet, seeing himself as an angel, can intuit a spiritual death and "renascence" which provide the true access to the life of the spirit.

The poem sent with "les Fenêtres" to Cazalis, "l'Assaut," which later became "le Château de l'Espérance" (Castle of Hope), was never published during Mallarmé's lifetime. But he took up its theme and movement twice again: five and then twenty-two years later, in "Quelle soie aux baumes de temps" (What silk embalmed by time). Here once again, thanks to the commentary accompanying the poem, we can glimpse at its birth the process of Mallarmé's inspiration. "From hair, which brought to my mind the idea of a flag . . ." The poet, full of amorous ardor, is struck by the analogy between the undulating hair of his beloved and the folds of a flag fluttering playfully in the sun. He surrenders to a movement of intoxication and conquest which announces from afar one of the components of "l'Après-midi d'un Faune" (Afternoon of a Faun). Thus the cardinal processes and functions of his poetry were gradually developing.

The conviction of the sacred character of poetry took an in-

creasing hold on Mallarmé, as it had on Gautier and the poets
of Art for Art's Sake. "Only art is true, immutable, great, and
sacred," he wrote at this time to Cazalis. From this point on,
he seems to have had a guilty conscience whenever he could
not devote himself entirely to his vocation. Whence ever more
stringent requirements upon what he produced and, as a corol-
lary, a growing hesitation to write a poem which might not be
perfect.

Thus the more he advanced in his career the more he limited
his production to "occasional verse," written, in a way, under
coercion. The year before, Cazalis had already asked him for
some lines in honor of Ettie, a lovely young Englishwoman
with whom he was madly in love. Mallarmé had answered,
"Let me have enough time. . . . I don't want this to be written
from sheer inspiration; lyricism's turbulence would be unworthy
of this chaste apparition you love. *Long meditation is necessary*;
only art, limpid and impeccable, is chaste enough to sculpt her
precisely." And finally, after long months and repeated entreaties from Cazalis, the chaste "Apparition," a complex product of the poet's temperament, life, and dreams, saw the light.

Mallarmé exhibits in this poem an ease and grace which he
never found again. This pure masterpiece of fluid musicality
combines an unconscious recollection of his dead sister, evoked
by the procession of white and seraphic images; a veiled allusion
to his own loves, often mingled with a voluptuous sadness; and
finally a luminous reference to the young Ettie, "la fée au
chapeau de clarté" (the fairy coifed in brightness). She is confused with the two silhouettes, viewed through a filigree of nostalgia, of the sister and the fiancée, and, in the distance, that
of a mother lost too soon. No doubt the emotion emanating
from these verses comes especially from the *complex* of feminine
images, intermingled in the poem as they were in Mallarmé's
subconscious. The expression of this complex is moving and
charming because the poet has gone beyond his own experience
and the urging of his temperament. He has been able to let his
most secret voice, the voice of his "anima," speak. Fusing dream
and reality into impalpable music, he has pierced somehow to
the very essence of love, the

>   *. . . parfum de tristesse*
> *Que même sans regret et sans déboire laisse*
> *La cueillaison d'un Rêve au coeur qui l'a cueilli.*

>   (. . . perfume of sadness
> Which, without regret or disappointment,
> The Dream that was plucked leaves to the very heart
>   that plucked it.)

II. THE ARRIVAL IN TOURNON. "L'AZUR"

At the end of the autumn of 1863, armed with a diploma
of aptitude in English, an appointment for the remainder of
the scholastic year to the Imperial Collège at Tournon, and a
young wife, Mallarmé took on his first position. Despite the
modesty of his salary (1200 francs a year), he had hoped that
freedom from material worries would enable him to devote his
leisure to what was gradually becoming his principal reason for
living: poetry. More than one poem sang in his head; and there
was also the translation of Poe, promised to the director of the
Revue Nouvelle, which was to be the opportunity for a closer
communion with the writer whom he already called his "grand
master" in poetry.

Unfortunately, he had to abandon these hopes rather rapidly.
Several days in a hotel, the move to a sordid apartment ("I
couldn't even find a place to live that wasn't a stable"), and
"the horrible wind that blows eternally through Tournon,"
and Mallarmé collapsed, "rigid with rheumatism and nailed to
an armchair." If only the forced rest had favored the return
of inspiration! On the contrary, it served only to bring back the
specter of impotency, as nagging as a fixation. The specter took
shape against the southern sky, that obsessive blue constantly
washed by the relentless mistral. He thought back with nostalgia
to the "dear fogs" of London and, as he had recently written
to Cazalis, "that immense circle, impalpable but real, behind
which beautiful scattered trees were feebly sketched." That
décor had at least helped him to forget the infinite distance of
his ideal dream. Now the sky seemed to him more inaccessible
and demanding than ever. The implacable blue became a symbol of eternity in his eyes, and its smile, the smile of "Renou-

veau," was charged with serene irony; its intense, reproving glance seemed meant to make the poet ashamed of having failed his vocation.

For the second time, Mallarmé faced the seemingly insoluble contradiction of having to create and being powerless to do it. Again, he attempted to win out by describing the contradiction. Now, however, it was no longer a question of describing, but of suggesting. The poet had spent a year in the school of Poe, who had taught him that in poetry "the first consideration of all is the effect to be produced." Like his master, Mallarmé banished from his new poem "a thousand lyrical affabilities" and sought at any price "the *effect produced*, without dissonance, without a single flourish" (to Cazalis, January 12, 1864). He took great pains to vanquish his "heartrending impotency," pains that were increased by the more severe conditions he was imposing on the realization of his idea.

On January 12, 1864, he sent Cazalis "l'Azur," finally finished. He enclosed a commentary which seems to elucidate its meaning: a true drama in which the poet, suffering from the cruel disease of impotency, flees from the blue that is torturing him and invokes the mists to help his escape. Then, "like a liberated schoolboy," he cries, "The sky is dead!" and, armed with this admirable certitude, he addresses his prayers to Matter. But the dead sky returns, singing in the blue bells, and obsession with it pierces the poet through and through.

The movement of "Fenêtres" is inverted here. Mallarmé no longer aspires to join the promise-filled blue beyond the fogs of England. He seeks on the contrary to flee it, recalling the mists for which he is now nostalgic. What else besides a kind of exasperation of his mystical sense could cause this reversal of attitude? Seeking to purify the old Dream, to rid it of all childhood imagery, Mallarmé seems suddenly stricken with fear. Can the Ideal be gazed upon, face to face, in its nakedness? And what does it become then, if not an immense emptiness, one of those "great blue holes maliciously made by the birds"?

At the presentiment that he was at the verge of metaphysical anguish, Mallarmé averted his eyes. He was not yet strong enough to brave the Absolute. For the moment, he could only deny it and try to forget the temptation of the blue. "The sky is dead!" Is that not the meaning of these words, which then seemed to him a "blasphemous boast"? He believed he could thus be delivered from his obsessions and, in a word, repress his mystical dreams. But his "death-throes" had just begun. His failure up until now to sever the absolute cleanly from his past dream caused the dream to triumph in its old form, in a great noise of bells and blue angeluses.

Although the poet was not liberated from his dream, nor from his impotency, he had at least affirmed the originality of his poetry. The *general effect* that he strove for was attained: the obsession with the eternal, symbolized by the blue. This was achieved through particular effects, all of which contributed to the general effect by metaphorically suggesting complex states of mind: sentences drawn out in arabesques over one or several stanzas, and interwoven syntax (already a first step toward hermeticism).[1] Networks of images were organized according to an outline which seems to reflect Mallarmé's intimate psyche: on the one hand, the ceiling which encloses, as in a prison, the vacant soul of a melancholy and impotent poet—a miry prison, filled with livid swamps and Lethean ponds; on the other, the blue, filled with bells, but "indolent as flowers." This last phrase will more than once help us to follow Mallarmé along his road.

"L'Azur," no matter what it seems, is already a difficult work, in which Mallarmé placed his first "fermoirs d'or" (golden closures) to disconcert, if not to discourage, importunate readers. His correspondent and admirer, Armand Renaud, was perhaps correct when he said of this poem that it was "sometimes obscure because of the lyricism."

[1] For example, the stanza:

> *Car j'y veux, puisque enfin ma cervelle, vidée*
> *Comme le pot de fard gisant au pied d'un mur,*
> *N'a plus l'art d'attifer la sanglotante idée,*
> *Lugubrement bâiller vers un trépas obscur.*

> For there I wish, since finally my brain, empty
> As a rouge jar lying at the foot of a wall,
> No longer has the art to bedizen the sobbing idea,
> To yawn lugubriously toward an obscure death.)

III. WATER AND MIRROR IMAGERY.

"LAS DE L'AMER REPOS," "LE PITRE CHÂTIÉ"

Yet these techniques were still nothing. Slowly, laboriously, during that interminable winter, in the midst of all the problems of a beginning teacher, Mallarmé put the finishing touches on his "system" and unceasingly meditated upon the poetic act. Through his many selfs he was seeking to discover his authentic personality.

His familiar demon of concentration and pitiless self-criticism probably suggested this recipe, soon sent to Cazalis:

One must always cut the beginning and the end of what one writes. No introduction, no conclusion. Do you think I'm crazy? Someday I'll explain to you that my madness lies elsewhere . . .

This simple sentence contains at least one key to Mallarmé's famous obscurity. From here on, ellipsis, telescoping, and metaphorical leaps became his favored instruments in the quest of the effect produced. He then combined them with the disjointed sentence which tended more and more to unroll its tangled scrolls—always apparently interrupted—into an arabesque running from beginning to end of the poem. The poem then became, as in "Las de l'amer repos" (Weary of the bitter rest), an almost single sentence of twenty-eight lines, in which several landscapes are skillfully superimposed. It was not merely a game. Faithful to his quest, Mallarmé saw a means of attaining a truer self in these successive substitutions of landscapes. A rejection, first of all, of his lazy childhood dream which turned him away from poetic work; but also a rejection of wearying, superhuman effort, of that fight against impotency, waged on so many sleepless nights, which finally took the form of a real intellectual suicide. Once again, in a resurgence of will, he tried to escape the death-agony before the lamp and, freed from all the constraints of his nature, to pluck the miraculous flower grafted on the "soul's blue filigree." Here is the landscape of his choice, blooming on some unknown bank as in a Chinese miniature:

Une ligne d'azur mince et pâle serait
Un lac, parmi le ciel de porcelaine nue,

Un clair croissant perdu par une blanche nue
Trempe sa corne calme en la glace des eaux,
Non loin de trois grands cils d'émeraude, roseaux.

(A thin and pale line of blue would be
A lake, within the sky of naked porcelain,
A clear crescent lost by a white cloud
Dips its calm tip into the mirror of the waters,
Not far from three great emerald eyelashes, reeds).

It is an evocation full of a delicate and rare preciosity, in which every object tends to become an allusion. As Poulet has perceptively noted, the blue gradually pales to become metamorphosed into a white night. A lake, a crescent moon, reeds fine as eyelashes: a landscape of immobile purity in which the blue, become simple line, fuses with the lake, become mirror. Reality tends to be identified with its own reflection.

Mallarmé abandoned himself to this play of mirrors during several months in an unending search for a definition of his poetry. In March of 1864 it dictated the stanzas of "le Pitre châtié" (The Punished Clown), in which the image of the lake (thanks to the presence of the reeds, which here again become eyelashes for the poet) is confused with the beloved's eyes. The theme of the clown and the mountebank had been "in the air" for a good many years. More precisely, this sonnet could be an echo of Baudelaire's prose poem, "le Vieux Saltimbanque"; it could also have been inspired by Poe's "Philosophy of Composition":

. . . the painful erasures . . . the wheels and pinions—the tackle for scene-shifting—the step-ladders, and demon-traps—the cock's feathers, the red paint and the black patches, which, in ninety-nine cases out of the hundred, constitute the properties of the literary *histrio.* . . .

But the roots of "le Pitre châtié" are planted in the depths of Mallarmé himself, in his eternal obsession with "bohemians strewn with stars" and the "mendieurs d'azur," the beggars of the blue.

At the same time, "le Pitre" offers the first image of the Poet that is really typical of Mallarmé as we have come to know him, much more precisely than "Contre un Poète parisien," "le Guignon," or "le Sonneur." The original version of this sonnet,

which Dr. Bonniot luckily found,[2] so different from the text
published in 1887, allows us to grasp in a nebulous state this
image and the metaphorical network in which it is inserted. It
should be examined closely.

The sonnet begins with a metaphorical leap, the intuition of
an analogy similar to that in "Château de l'Espérance" and im-
plicit in the last line of "Las de l'amer repos":

> *Non loin de trois grands cils d'émeraude, roseaux.*

If reeds are to the lake what lashes are to the eyes, then a hidden
correspondence exists between an eye and a lake. One "plunges"
into both, sometimes in exaltation. Mallarmé will suggest this
in the second stanza, having first taken care to entwine the two
systems of images to obtain the effect of "superimposition" that
we saw in rough form in the preceding poem:

> *Pour ses yeux,—pour nager dans ces lacs, dont les quais*
> *Sont plantés de beaux cils qu'un matin bleu pénètre . . .*

> (For her eyes,—to swim in these lakes whose banks
> Are planted with beautiful lashes that a blue morning
> penetrates . . .)

The image awaits the telescoping that took place twenty-three
years later in the simple juxtaposition of the two words which
led scholars astray for a long time: "Yeux, lacs . . ."

It is not just any bather or any lover plunging, diving into the
waters. It is the Poet, who, with his customary lucidity, knows
full well that he is only a clown, the Muse's clown. And why
does he dive? Because he is tired of that room where the lamp
of inspiration smokes and flickers, which has become the Muse's
"baraque où fument les quinquets" (hovel where the oil lamps
smoke). Thus the superimposition is not double, but triple.
The image of the Poet, fleeing his condition of poet-clown, the
Muse's tyranny, and poetic creation, is substituted for the image
of the lover about to plunge into his beloved's eyes, which had
first been superimposed on the image of the bather. And the
Poet, to do this, dares this time to accomplish the act presented
in "Fenêtres" only as a postulation: he leaps out of the window,

2 *Oeuvres complètes*, p. 1414.

contemptuously ignoring the Muse's call, forgetting his clown's garb as well as his poet's craft. He surrenders to the intoxication of bathing naked in "l'onde aux blancs galets" (the white-pebbled waters), feeling a new body, healthier and as if purified by the water, which seems to make the coolness of snows and glaciers penetrate his whole body. He has then finally yielded to the call of the blue, to that thirst for purity which "Fenêtres" already expressed. Thanks to the "blue morning," he could be reborn; the anterior sky has somehow come down to earth to be identified with the water, which had only been its mirror until now. For the first time, he has been able to live out, truly and almost physically, his dream of purity, in a pagan joy expressed by the very movement of the sonnet. Its images and verses ring out like a hymn of deliverance. Yet, even in his intoxication, Mallarmé has a kind of guilty conscience, for he senses perfectly well that he is a "traitor" to his vocation when bathing in the pure water of the dream. He does not yet quite know why. But something deep within him tells him that genius is a garment, that poetry is made of rouge and greasepaint (Poe had said, "red paint and black patches"), that a naked poet is no longer a poet, and that, finally, pure poetry is perhaps only a mirage and an illusion.

Thus the values of Mallarmé's fundamental obsessions are specified with regard to the poetic act. To flee the room or the hovel, to break the windowpane, to yield to the intoxication of water, fire, or the blue, is in any case to defy a prohibition ("these forbidden lakes") and at the same time to be false to his poet's condition. Torn between the ideal and the real, his *vocation* is to transmute the latter into the former.

His first masters in poetry taught him this. When, after hours of battling with the Muse, he came upon the same obsession with impotency again, "the hatred of creation and the sterile love of nothingness," he turned to those who had once opened the gates of heaven for him: Gautier, Baudelaire, Banville. They were particularly dear to him not only because they were in his eyes the greatest poets, but also because he recognized an aspect of himself in each of them. An instinctive need for introspection and examination of conscience as much as the desire to render a striking homage to his masters led him in April, 1864, to write three prose poems, published in *l'Artiste* the following year as "Symphonie littéraire." The inner reason for this did not escape the notice of his friend Lefébure, who wrote on May 13, 1864: ". . . I mean that in painting them, you have painted yourself, and that you have put four poets into three. . . ."

Mallarmé admired the "impeccable artist" in Gautier, whom Baudelaire had already honored in his famous dedication, the poet whose lucidity and mysterious word-science had opened up for him the intimate harmony of colors and the profound treasure of correspondences. The Mallarmé who wrote "L'hiver, saison de l'art serein, l'hiver lucide" (Winter, season of serene art, lucid winter) could hardly resist a poet who had, in his words, reached *"the highest summit of serenity,* where we are ravished by beauty."

It was other charms that attracted Mallarmé to Baudelaire. From his very first reading of *les Fleurs du Mal,* he had been strangely struck to find his own inner landscape. It was "a surprising landscape," with its dead waters, its sky livid with boredom, and, here and there, in the splendor of a beautiful October sunset, some wing-feathers of fallen souls and the grace of faded things. Then too there was the bitter feeling of exile that Mallarmé had experienced so often in contemplating the sky, and the Baudelairean revelation of a mystical native country where saints carry palms, and angels' harps unite with cymbals of native gold. But it is to be noted that here, except for a discreet allusion to Satin (whom he draws as a mountebank), Mallarmé instinctively retains only those Baudelairean images that had become familiar to his own poetry, thus proving that he was trying through others to define himself.

If in his heart of hearts he seems to have particularly cherished Banville, it is because the latter brought him a justification of sorts for his penchant toward lyricism, against which he had been struggling for two years in the name of a will to lucidity. For Banville is the very voice of the lyre, and his word is the cry of a soul drunk with glory:

> *Tout ce qu'il y a d'enthousiasme ambrosien en moi et de bonté musicale, de noble et de pareil aux dieux, chante, et j'ai l'extase radieuse de la Muse! J'aime les roses, j'aime l'or du soleil, j'aime les harmonieux sanglots des femmes aux longs cheveux, et je voudrais tout confondre dans un poétique baiser!* ("Symphonie littéraire")

(Everything in me that partakes of ambrosian enthusiasm, of musical goodness, of nobility, of godhood, sings, and I feel the radiant ecstasy of the Muse! I love roses, I love the sun's gold, I love the harmonious sobs of women with their long hair, *and I would like to mingle them all in a poetic kiss!*)

Let us remember this act of faith, for Mallarmé would never again write such an avowal of what he could have been, nor such a hymn to the Muse and to love. It is remarkable to discover in the "Symphonie littéraire" what seems to be a more precise response to the piece he had sent previously to his friend des Essarts, "Contre un Poète parisien" (Against a Parisian Poet). There was more here than an homage to his initiators: an adieu to lyricism, a sort of psychoanalysis of "the pleasures of a passive soul, still only a woman and perhaps to be a beast tomorrow," unless the soul were to succeed in vanquishing its obsessions and realizing, like Gautier, the absolutely new poetry he was dreaming of, although he could not imagine exactly what it would be.

IV. THE BIRTH OF "HÉRODIADE"

In fact, Mallarmé had not yet done with his familiar demons. Without knowing the "Symphonie littéraire," one could believe that after "le Pitre châtié" Mallarmé had reached a certain serenity by 1864. But two other poems of the same period, "Angoisse" (Anxiety) and the first version of "Tristesse d'été" (Summer Sadness), are in flat contradiction to this impression. Although the movement of flight is apparently analogous, here the poet seeks refuge no longer in the woman's eyes, but in her mass of hair, and asks the "lukewarm stream" not for a rebirth in purity but for a plunge into nothingness and self-oblivion. Traces of Baudelaire are certainly in evidence here, but also the return of old torments which, linked with the obsession with death, gave rise to a theme destined henceforth to occupy a great deal of Mallarmé's thought and poetry: the theme of nothingness, "le néant."

In truth, what had life brought him? A trying profession which required the endless repetition of grammatical rules to indifferent, stupid, or mocking boys; a life in the provinces, where one sank bit by bit into insignificance; material worries which constantly disturbed the intimacy of his home. "Every

day discouragement overcomes me, I am dying of torpor. I
shall come out of this stupefied and voided. I feel like beating
my head against the wall to wake up" (to Cazalis, Holy
Wednesday, 1864).

Yet these were only advance symptoms of the crisis. There
were days when the poet's pain was more discreet. It melted, as
in "Soupir" (Sigh), into a sweetly melancholy landscape, where
the blue of the sky—the tender azure of October—tended to
become more and more identified with its own reflection in
the dead water. Or else, as in "Fleurs" (Flowers), the poet en-
folded his pain in the great cups of the flowers that he loved.
Gladioli, lilies, and roses seemed to him to bear witness to a
primordial purity, fallen long ago from "des avalanches d'or du
vieil azur" (the golden avalanches of the ancient blue). Among
them a newcomer suddenly appeared, clothed in her wild
nakedness, "Hérodiade en fleur du jardin clair" (Hérodiade
as a flower of the bright garden).

Here we must stop a moment. April, 1864: At twenty-two,
Mallarmé had already accumulated a poetic backlog which to
other, less exacting poets would have amply justified the publication of a slim volume that might lead to glory, or at least to
success. Even his most critical friends attested to the value of
his poetry in the warmest of letters. Lefébure wrote him on
April 15:

What is especially striking in your dazzling and somber verses is
a singular power of concentration. It is probable that the reasons
for it go back very far in your life and have finally become a corol-
lary to the spleen which gives you your strength as a poet and your
sorrow as a man. . . . The handling and assiduous working-over
of a single thought which you squeeze until the last drop of juice
is extracted, the stubborn incubation and the steady labor: these,
I think, form the base of your talent. . . .

In his turn, Catulle Mendès, already a businessman of letters
at twenty-three, and still hoping to become the head of a new
poetic movement, urged him gently to "produce":

Must you isolate yourself in silence? And when one has written
such pieces as "les Fleurs" and a line like "Où rougit la pudeur des
aurores foulées" (where the modesty of trampled dawns blushes),
shouldn't one take advantage of one's talent and sing a little bit
for joy?

And yet Mallarmé had published nothing since the rare poems of 1862 which had appeared in *le Papillon, l'Artiste,* and *le Journal des Baigneurs* of Dieppe. Even though he had been in possession of the key to his poetry for two years, even though he had found several of the techniques which would permit him to create a work in no way similar to any other, he was conscious that he was not yet master of these means. Up to this point he had done nothing but seek himself and sing of himself. Every poem from "le Sonneur" to "Soupir" was in the first person. He who wanted to flee lyricism by focusing his lucid attention on the mystery of the poetic act had been no more able than others to escape subjective poetry. As he himself said later, the pieces he had written were only "so many revealing intuitions of his temperament." His images were certainly personal, but he saw clearly that they were a natural consequence of his personality, that he was not in control of them; they were not arranged according to a necessity inherent to them, because he had not yet plumbed the depths of his thought.

So he had to extricate himself from his work, put space between it and him, project outside of himself a creation capable of living through its own strength. His principal character would be imposed on him only by its mere presence, just as the "Phénomène futur" (Future Phenomenon) is imposed, in his modest canvas house, on the "Exhibitor of past things," who says:

J'apporte, vivante . . . , une Femme d'autrefois. . . . Quelque folie, originelle et naïve, une extase d'or, je ne sais quoi! par elle nommé sa chevelure, se ploie avec la grâce des étoffes autour d'un visage qu'éclaire la nudité sanglante de ses lèvres. À la place du vêtement vain, elle a un corps; et les yeux, semblables aux pierres rares, ne valent pas ce regard qui sort de sa chair heureuse: des seins levés comme s'ils étaient pleins d'un lait éternel, la pointe vers le ciel, aux jambes lisses qui gardent le sel de la mer première ("Poèmes en prose").

(I bring, living, a Woman of olden times. Some original and naïve madness, a golden ecstasy, I don't know what!—which she calls her hair, folds with the grace of cloth about a face illuminated by the bleeding nudity of her lips. In the place of useless clothing, she has a body; and her eyes, like precious stones, are no equals for that glance which springs from her radiant body: her breasts lifted as if they were full of an eternal milk, lifted toward the sky, her smooth legs still covered with the salt of the primeval sea.)

Mallarmé had his character already. Hérodiade, enigmatic and solitary, had arisen from the garden of his dream. In October, 1864, as another academic year began, he confided his ambitious project to Cazalis:

As for me, I am resolutely at work. I have finally begun "Hérodiade." In terror, for I am inventing a language that must necessarily spring from a very new poetics, which I could define in these few words: *to paint, not the thing, but the effect it produces*. The poetic line should be composed not of words but of intentions, and all words should efface themselves before sensations. I *mean*— for the first time in my life—*to succeed*. I would never pick up a pen again if I failed.

He was pledging himself to a decisive match, not yet suspecting the importance of what was at stake.

3 · The Death-Agony of the "Dream"

Quand l'ombre menaça de la fatale loi
Tel vieux Rêve, désir et mal de mes vertèbres,
Affligé de périr sous les plafonds funèbres
Il a ployé son aile indubitable en moi
"SONNET"

(When darkness threatened with the fatal law
An old Dream, the desire and pain of my ver-
tebrae,
Sorrowful at dying under funereal ceilings
It folded its indubitable wing within me.)

I. THE SCENARIO OF "HÉRODIADE"

Mallarmé began the tragedy "Hérodiade" in October, 1864. He had in hand a theme cherished for a long time: the heroine whose thirst for purity makes her reject life, the perfect symbol of Mallarmé's poetry. For the moment, this notion was merely a systematized transposition of Poe's. However, his thought had evolved in the ensuing months. He was no longer concerned, as in "l'Azur," with the "effect produced" by the poem on the reader, which was still only a writer's technique of paying particular attention to the conditions of success in the best sense of the word. He was now concerned with the effect produced by the thing itself, on men in general and the poet in particular—therefore with a subjective intuition of reality, a *poetic attitude* already assuming, at least implicitly, that true reality is situated beyond all expression.

Consequently, his "very new poetics" was in the service of an equally new subject. He had certainly not entirely invented this subject. Without necessarily referring, with Thibaudet, to the sonnet in which Baudelaire paints "the cold majesty of the sterile woman," one can think, for instance, of Flaubert's *Salammbô*, published more than a year previously, and of Villier de l'Isle-Adam's Isis, a cold and enigmatic creature who had very much struck Mallarmé and may well have oriented him toward his subject. What would be new in the creation of "Hérodiade" was his manner of identifying himself with the work. It was no longer a lyrical testimony of personal torment, nor a means of expression, but a means of research and self-discovery.

"Tu vis! ou vois-je ici l'ombre d'une princesse?" ("You live! or do I see here the shadow of a princess?") At the outset, "Hérodiade" poses the essential problem through the nurse's voice: the nature of life and death.[1] Up to this moment, the heroine has not ceased "walking in an unknown age," living through the Dream in an immemorial past, in the "siècles fauves" (wild centuries) and the "parfum désert" (solitary perfume) of former kings. In this regard, she is truly the flower fallen once upon a time from the "golden avalanches of the ancient blue," as she was in "les Fleurs." Nostalgic for a vague, lost paradise, she is now reduced to silently plucking the petals of the "pale lilies" within her. Careful to preserve the purity of this dying ideal, she will pitilessly repel the advances of the nurse, who will attempt three times to call her back to life: by a kiss, through the intoxication of perfumes, and, finally, with the simple gesture of arranging her hair. Impious solicitations! For Hérodiade has renounced life with all its impurity. The poet of "Tristesse d'Été" had already spoken of "hating life and feverish love" (in the text of 1864), with their processions of perfume and caresses. And now Hérodiade refuses:

> Ce baiser, ces parfums offerts et, le dirai-je?
> O mon coeur, cette main encore sacrilège . . .

(This kiss, these proffered perfumes and, shall I say it?
Oh my heart, this still sacrilegious hand . . .)

What then does she want? The nurse asks her,

> Pour qui, dévorée
> D'angoisses, gardez-vous la splendeur ignorée
> Et le mystère vain de votre être?

(For whom, devoured
By anguish, are you keeping the unknown splendor
And the vain mystery of your being?)

In truth, Mallarmé knew no better than she. To discover it, during the long winter watches he endlessly questioned his own

1 Commentary: Thibauet, pp. 269, 387. Noulet, pp. 97, 369. Mauron, pp. 45, 105; II, p. 120. Gengoux, p. 132.

image in the little Venetian mirror "deep as a cold fountain," mentioned in a prose poem of the same period, "Frisson d'hiver" (Winter Shiver).

After long hours punctuated by the rackets and hazings of the lycée, in the midst of the new baby's wails, which, he said, "cracked his skull," relentlessly he set about his work. In an exhausting struggle by lamplight, each night he tried to *live* every impression before translating it.

> O miroir!
> Eau froide par l'ennui dans ton cadre gelée
> Que de fois et pendant des heures, désolée
> Des songes et cherchant mes souvenirs qui sont
> Comme des feuilles sous ta glace au trou profond,
> Je m'apparus en toi comme une ombre lointaine.

> (Oh mirror!
> Cold water frozen by ennui in your frame
> How often and how long, driven desperate
> By dreams and searching my memories which are
> Like leaves under the ice of your deep depths,
> I appeared in you like a distant shadow.)

"Cold water frozen by boredom," "dreams like leaves": Mallarmé had really found, as he wrote to Cazalis in March, 1865,

. . . an intimate and singular manner of painting and noting fleeting impressions. Add, for more terror, that all these "impressions" follow each other as in a symphony, and I often spend whole days wondering if one can accompany another, what their relationship and their effect are. . . . You can imagine that I write few lines in a week.

When successful, this work resulted in a dense and sustained poetry with a resonance absolutely unheard of until then, but also in a true feeling of "terror" for the poet. For each line was now a sort of revelation for him:

> Mais, horreur! des soirs, dans ta sévère fontaine,
> J'ai de mon rêve épars connu la nudité!

> (But, horror! on some evenings in your severe fountain
> I have known the nudity of my disordered dream.)

Mallarmé confided to Cazalis: "In some instances, my lines hurt and wound like steel." Indeed, having dug so deeply into his dream to purify it, Mallarmé had gradually emptied it of its content. Farewell to the angels and cherubim of his childhood, the perfumed and nonchalant rivers of his adolescent reveries! "I want nothing human," says Hérodiade. To want to be pure is to die to the world.

> Oui, c'est pour moi, pour moi, que je fleuris, déserte!

> (Yes, it's for me, for myself, that I flower in solitude!)

But is this not also dying to oneself? "Madam, are you then going to die?" asked the agonized nurse, while Mallarmé, alone in his room and still focusing on the mirror, feels life withdraw from him:

> I drag myself around like an old man and I spend hours observing in mirrors the encroachment of torpor which is already dimming my eyes with their drooping lashes and making my mouth sag (to Cazalis, February, 1865).

Slowly he felt his ancient dreams vanish and burst like bubbles. They were just so many Épinal images, good at best for children. Having rejected all easy escapes as he had rejected all the temptations of sensual love and life, putting away, with his heroine, "the supreme and stifled sobs" of childhood, he *awaited*, as she did, "an unknown thing." No doubt it would be severe, difficult, and cold, but glittering and profoundly rich, a new ideal that he could not yet clearly define. It would be built on the debris of the old one and of pure gold, separated from base lead by a real transmutation. Scarcely quit of that childhood, he felt with Hérodiade

> . . . parmi les rêveries
> Se séparer enfin ses froides pierreries.[1]

> (. . . among the reveries
> [His] cold gems finally separated out.)

1 I cannot accept here J. Gengoux's interpretation (*op. cit.*, p. 146): "Alone, Hérodiade finally admits that she is vanquished. Her lips were lying: they were rejecting the supreme and stifled sobs of a childhood which, among its reveries, sensed the dissolution of its dream of absolute purity and the approach of the warmth of love." Everything in this poem seems to me to prove her passage to a superior state, from a childhood imprisoned by reveries to a maturity seeking not love but a new ideal.

So, in writing the scenario of "Hérodiade" at the cost of countless meditations, Mallarmé caught a glimpse of a terrible truth: Beauty is death, or at least something analogous: an inhuman white night, similar to the starry sky where innumerable diamonds shine, useless and vain. Earthly beauty, symbolized by Hérodiade, is merely a pale reflection, ready to be obliterated at the first contact, for it exists only through its perfume, which clothes it like a chalice.

II. THE APPEARANCE OF THE FAUN

As his friend Lefébure once remarked, Mallarmé was essentially a seasonal person. Periods of exaltation and depression, phases of tension and relaxation alternated in him as in nature. After many long and sleepless winter nights spent over "Hérodiade" by the "solitary light of the lamp," the spring of 1865 recalled him to milder dreams. The old temptations reappeared. Intoxication and flight dictated "Brise marine" (Sea Breeze)— a last echo of Baudelairean escape.

> *Fuir! Là-bas fuir! Je sens que les oiseaux sont ivres*
> *D'être parmi l'écume inconnue et les cieux!*

(To flee! to flee far away! I feel that the birds are drunk
From being amid the unknown foam and the skies!)

It was a farewell to his childhood dreams, the final concession to the lyricism he had finally killed in himself. He scarcely heard the call of the sea again until the end of his life, when, in a tragic décor of storms and shipwrecks, he wrote "Un Coup de Dés." But in "Brise marine" there seems to be a kind of presentiment of future disaster:

> *Et, peut-être, les mâts, invitant les orages*
> *Sont-ils de ceux qu'un vent penche sur les naufrages . . .*

(And perhaps the masts inviting storms
Are of the kind that a wind inclines toward shipwrecks . . .)

Be that as it may, "Brise marine" awakened in him the themes of fire, intoxication, and desire. Shortly thereafter, they inspired him to an important new poem, the summer's answer to "Hérodiade":

I have been at work for ten days. I have left "Hérodiade" for
the cruel winter: That solitary work had sterilized me, and in the
interval I am rhyming an heroic interlude with a *Faun* as its hero"
(to Cazalis, June, 1865.)

This first version of Mallarmé's future masterpiece has been
rediscovered: the "Monologue du Faune" [2] (The Faun's Monologue), written in less than three months, an exceptional tour
de force for Mallarmé. It was probably influenced by Banville's
"Diane au bois" (Diana in the Woods). One-act plays were in
vogue and, were Mallarmé to write one, Banville had undertaken to present it at the Comédie Française. The prospect of
being performed stimulated Mallarmé. The Faun now "had him
by the hair" and allowed him no respite. He contrived its attitude and the stage business, and applied himself to "writing
original verses" which would be "absolutely theatrical."

He was, in fact, still trying to understand himself. He commented that his Faun, a new aspect of his own personality, was
at grips with "a very lofty and beautiful idea" which had to be
elucidated. While adjusting a reed on his flute, the Faun sur-
prises through the leaves a "flight of naiads" who are running
away, startled. Not all flee, however, for in the deep shade he
discovers two of them sleeping, entwined in the "ecstasy of
being two." He seizes them cautiously and carries them in his
arms toward sunny gardens, where he tries to possess them. But,
slipping from his grasp, the two nymphs suddenly disappear.
Now everything has returned to silence. The Faun remains
alone with his memories. What has happened? Are they really
memories? Or was it only an "illusion of his fabulous senses,"
an effect of his torrid desire? He refuses to believe it and finally
succumbs to sleep.

Hérodiade had received a counterpart: she who was so shy
had found her complement, the "bad girl," the "sister who
bursts into flame," all ardor and love. Cold and heat, icy reserve
and overflowing sensuality: would Mallarmé's two halves be
joined and reconciled through the "Faun's Monologue"?

They had almost joined, and such was precisely the sin, the
crime, committed by the Faun: to have wanted to possess the

2 Commentary: Noulet, p. 228. Gengoux, p. 148.

nymphs. To do so, he had to choose between them and trouble their ecstatic love, that "cluster of kisses so well commingled by the gods." By his desire he had divided something once whole, while at the same time defiling the purity that Hérodiade wanted to preserve at any price. Here we can grasp the "lofty and beautiful idea" which presided over the composition of the monologue: the problem of dream and reality. Man occasionally thinks he sees his dreams materialize, believes that he can embrace the object of his desires. But in that very embrace the dream's purity is injured, the object vanishes, and only the memory remains. Can it be, then, that all reality is merely illusion? We are not yet at that point. Simply, as earlier in "Tristesse d'Été," Mallarmé/the Faun, having surrendered to the intoxication of the world, to the "high sun, father of wines" and to kindled flesh, is content to ask deep slumber to erase the memory of his disappointments.

III. THE DEMON OF ANALOGY

Banville and Coquelin liked the poetry of my "Faun" enormously but felt that it lacked the action demanded by the public and assured me that only poets would be interested. . . . I am relegating my subject to a drawer for several months, to be freely rewritten later . . . and I am beginning "Hérodiade," no longer a tragedy but a poem [for the same reasons?], particularly because I thus acquire the whole attitude, the costumes, the décor, and the furnishings, not to speak of the mystery. For this I am going to accustom my rebellious temperament to nocturnal labor, since the wretches who pay me at school plunder my best hours" (to Cazalis, November, 1865).

Mallarmé was not, then, discouraged by the lack of understanding—or the wisdom—of his Parisian friends. He merely drew conclusions from his failure. Why persist in writing for the theater when it meant being confined to so many conditions and limitations? Settled in a more comfortable new apartment pleasantly overlooking the Rhône and the hills beyond, he lightheartedly went back to work in October, 1865, resolved to triumph over the rigors of school and prepared to relinquish sleep in order to do so. "Spleen has almost deserted me and my poetry has risen from its debris."

Happy to be able at last to create surroundings to his con-

venience and taste, he slowly allowed his fantasy free course.
The severe living room with its deep chest and small Saxon
clock was soon enlivened by graceful fauna: a white cat, a gold-
fish, and a bluebird, which brought joy to little Geneviève and
pleased the slightly precious taste of the poet.

But this euphoria did not last very long. The lengthy sessions
of night work, that sad price of a harassing profession, returned
shortly with "Hérodiade." Soon he was writing to Cazalis: "An
atrocious neuralgia was pounding my temples, twisting the
nerves in my teeth, day and night; during moments of respite,
I would throw myself like a desperate maniac on my poem's
unattainable Overture; it is singing inside my head, but I can
not get it down . . ."

While awaiting inspiration, Mallarmé tried to suggest in a
few lines the impression he had experienced after having finished the scenario of "Hérodiade:"

> *Je t'apporte l'enfant d'une nuit d'Idumée*
>
> (I bring you the child of an Idumaean night).

This first line of "Don du Poème" (Gift of the Poem) has
caused much ink to flow.[3] Yet to explain it does not necessitate
going all the way back to the Cabala—of which Mallarmé to all
appearances was totally ignorant at this point—nor to the pre-
Adamic kings of Idumaea. As Mauron has pointed out, Idumaea
is, simply, the name of the land where "Hérodiade" takes place.

The poem's theme is simple. After a night of fierce labor by
lamplight, the poet discovers his work at dawn in its true light.
Although he judges it now without indulgence, he brings it to
his wife, who is rocking the baby Geneviève, so that she may
give some of her milk also to the newborn infant of poetry. The
poem's composition is less simple; it even disconcerted Aubanel
when Mallarmé sent the poem to him. One sentence unfolds
throughout the fourteen lines in an almost constant arabesque.
Through his choice of words, the poet seeks increasingly, not
objects, but the sensations they evoke. Thus dawn becomes a
sort of plucked bird with a pallid and bleeding wing; the mater-

---

3 Commentary: Saurat: *Perspectives,* p. 113. Noulet, p. 397. Mauron,
p. 104.

nal voice, a sound of viola and harpsichord; the poem, a suckling babe made hungry by the "air of the virgin blue" where he was born. The images, not new in Mallarmé, are here strangely super-imposed and combined in a network. The key to this singular conception is to be found in a prose poem which seems to have been written at precisely the same time: "le Démon de l'Ana-logie" (The Demon of Analogy).

Here Mallarme reveals the secret of what he too could call the "genesis of a poem." First of all, an unexpected sensation: "La sensation d'une aile glissant sur les cordes d'un instru-ment" (the sensation of a wing drawn across the strings of an instrument), i.e., the intuition of an analogy between a wing and a musician's bow. Then, immediately, an unknown phrase singing on his lips, "lambeau maudit d'une phrase absurde" (an accursed fragment of an absurd sentence), comes to "re-place" the impression of a sliding wing and is perceived as a fragment of verse, one part being for the rhyme, the other for the beginning of the next line: "La Pénultième / Est morte" (the penultimate one is dead). The poet then leaves his home; and while he is walking in the street the two sensations gradu-ally melt into each other, seeking a justification of their pe-culiar birth. The sound of "nul" (nothing) becomes first the sound of the taut string. Then it is the entire Penultimate, a word probably dictated by Mallarmé the grammarian, which is confused with a personified string that breaks and for which the poet begins to wear mourning. "La Pénultième est morte, elle est morte, bien morte, la désespérée Pénultième" (The Penultimate is dead, she is dead, quite dead, the despairing Pe-nultimate). Even more, he catches himself imitating with his hand "the gesture of a caress that is stroking something." All that was seemingly only a strange premonition, for, suddenly lifting his eyes, he notices that he is in front of a lute-maker's shop, which has old instruments hanging on the wall and palm leaves and old birds' wings on the floor!

However we choose to explain this confluence—premonition, chance, or perhaps a habit that brought him back to that same shop through some unconscious predilection—it matters little. Now we can grasp the principle of his poetic vision. First, in-spiration or the outside world furnishes him spontaneously with

complexes of words or images which he combines and super-
imposes, and from which he brings out *analogies* allowing the
discovery of their *reciprocal* meanings. Henceforth this polyvalence of images governed his manner of writing and became
the key to his poetry.

The combined images of the wing and the ancient instrument
reappeared two months later, in December, 1865, in another
"occasional" poem that he sent to a friend: "Sainte Cécile
jouant sur l'aile d'un chérubin" (St. Cecilia Playing on a
Cherub's Wing), later to become "Sainte." This time, a
stained-glass window depicting a saint and an angel suggests the
analogy between instruments and the cherub's wing. Charles
Mauron has noted that "the poem is constructed like a
diptych." True, but one must add that the two panels of the
diptych are superimposed in a sort of double exposure. The
Saint, with her viola and missal, initially evokes the splendors
of another time. The gold sparkling in the window is like the
Magnificat's sonorous passage in church at the hour of prayer.
But this evocation of an ancient dream becomes jumbled: it is
only a stained-glass window with vanished contours, where the
Saint now seems no longer to be singing to the viola but to be
playing the harp on the wing of the angel by her side, and
where the ancient music has become quasi-silence.

This admirable poem has been compared to an Italian "An-
nunciation." Here again, the design of its lines in an arabesque
of a single sentence has the delicacy of a primitive painting.
In addition, the choice of words and sonorities gives the design
a translucent musicality which, in this precious and somewhat
melancholy evocation of the past, is reminiscent of the English
Pre-Raphaelites. Mallarmé is more and more attentive to the
expressive aspect of each sound—suggesting the winged flight
of the angel by using soft labial consonants; the sound of the
viola and the harp through a subtle play between dentals and
combined liquids; and the broad resonance of canticles in the
balance between the sounds "a" and "an." He especially suc-
ceeds in the last stanza, where the smothered murmur of sibilant
sounds and "i's" really expresses silence. For Mallarmé himself,
it was a "little melodic poem, composed especially with music
in mind."

There is more to be said. This poem not only contains a supremely nostalgic evocation of the old Dream that had haunted his childhood and youth with its cherubim, its grazing wings and streaming gold, and its trace of a real complex about a maternal breast charged with mystical values. It also contains a sort of presentiment of the poet's future esthetic and is the first attempt at transmuting his old dream into a poetry of silence and absence. The gold has vanished; there are no longer, as there once were, an old book, sandalwood; there is only the image of a Saint playing in silence upon the wing of the ideal.

IV. "L'OUVERTURE ANCIENNE" (THE ANCIENT OVERTURE)

At this time, Mallarmé was spending the winter nights laboring over the Overture to "Hérodiade." Living, as he put it, "in inviolate solitude and silence," seeking "an unknown oblivion so as to hear the song of certain mysterious notes within," he occasionally confided his hopes and dreams to his friends. "Ah! this poem," he wrote to Cazalis, "I want it to come out a magnificent jewel from the sanctuary of my thought, or I will expire on its debris! Having only the night hours to myself, I spend them dreaming of all the words in advance."

He allowed only a few days' interruption to attend his grandfather's funeral in Versailles. On the way back, he dropped in on his friends in Paris, who all entertained him. Along with Catulle Mendès, the founder of the first *Parnasse contemporain*, he saw its principal contributors: Banville, Cazalis, Coppée, Xavier de Ricard. Mallarmé took advantage of his brief stay to correct the proofs of poems he had sent to Mendès for their anthology. Finding it impossible to join Marie and Geneviève for the Christmas holidays, he contented himself perforce with sending them several little presents; and he decided to take part in the festivities to which Leconte de Lisle himself had given him a friendly invitation. There he was, in the first ranks of the poets of his day. His own greatness was enhanced by the distance and mystery with which he already surrounded his work.

Upon his return, he went back to his slow and painful labors. He was absorbed in trying to feel "extraworldly impressions" and creating an absolutely new poetry. In March came an

illumination: "I was fortunate enough last night to see my
Poem again in its nudity, and I mean to attempt the Work this
evening." A cry of triumph followed soon thereafter: "I have
spent three months straining over 'Hérodiade,' my lamp can
attest to that. . . . I have written the musical 'Overture.' " But
it was also a cry of distress, for the now famous letter to Cazalis
(March, 1866) continues:

> Unfortunately, in delving so deeply in my verse I have run into
> two abysses that reduce me to despair. One is Nothingness, where
> I have arrived without being acquainted with Buddhism, and I
> am still too wretched to be able to believe even in my own poetry
> and return to the work that this crushing thought has made me
> abandon.
> Yes, I *know*, we are merely vain forms of matter—but truly sub-
> lime for having invented God and our soul. So sublime, my friend!
> that I mean to take on this spectacle of matter, which is aware of
> being and yet flings itself passionately into the Dream that it knows
> does not exist, singing of the Soul and of all the other equally
> divine impressions we have amassed since the earliest ages, and
> proclaiming before the Nothing that is truth, these glorious lies!
> Such is the plan of my lyrical volume and perhaps its title: *The
> Glory of the Lie* or *The Glorious Lie*. I will sing as one who has
> lost hope.

Thus, there is no doubt: it was in writing "l'Ouverture ancienne" and in "delving so deeply in his verse" that he encountered Nothingness, "le Néant." From now on, the poetic
experience was fused for him with metaphysical experience,
and the "Overture" should be read as a document of that terri-
fying descent into the depths of despair.

His point of departure was the familiar setting evoked in the
"Don du Poème" and the same disquieting hour, when dawn's
first wan glimmer chases away the anxieties, but also the dreams,
of the night. The customary images—the wing, the angel, gold,
glass—take on an even more tragic cast. For here the Dawn
(identified simultaneously with a bird of vain black plumage,
the angel of the dream, and finally the poet's soul) is bound
to that sensation of falling which had obsessed him two years
earlier, appearing in the last line of "Fenêtres," in "Plainte
d'Automne," and in "le Démon de l'Analogie." Here we see

Mallarmé's process taking firm shape: The images are crystallized through superimpressions which suggest analogies, and the network of metaphors is organized simultaneously on several levels, conferring on the description of a landscape a personal as well as a quasi-universal meaning.

> *Abolie, et son aile affreuse dans les larmes*
> *Du bassin, aboli, qui mire les alarmes . . .*

> (Abolished, and her frightful wing in the tears
> Of the pond, abolished, which reflects alarm . . .)

One word reverberated in Mallarmé's mind: "aboli," abolished; and immediately networks of images surged forth from his subconscious: the "unforgettable swan" of "les Fenêtres" and "les Fleurs," dawn with her vain black plumage projecting sinister reflections in the water, golden and dark red palm leaves, and, in an even more subterranean manner, the angel mirrored in "les Fenêtres." Angel, bird, dawn, and the poet's soul are all associated. Now comes the final struggle with the bygone Baudelairean and mystical dream, the old "plumage," God, as he would say later. The dream has just been consumed in a purple sky as if on a burning pyre, its reflection fading gradually in the grim water of the pool.

> *Crime! bûcher! aurore ancienne! supplice!*
> *Pourpre d'un ciel! Étang de la pourpre complice!*

> (Crime! pyre! ancient dawn! torture!
> Crimson sky! pool, accomplice of the crimson!)

The Nurse, helpless, attends Hérodiade's "torture." Hérodiade is incapable of attaining purity except through the sacrifice of all her childhood reveries—a torture that is at the same time an intellectual suicide, a "crime," for the princess in her sad manor house is no longer sovereign of anything but "fallen lands."

Then, called forth by the words "plumage" and "wing," a new image is sketched in another superimpression: the stained-glass window saint, with her train of sacerdotal objects and her finger, that subtle musician. The window enters here as if to assure the passage between two worlds: the external landscape of dawn, the pool, sky, fallen lands; and the world of the "singular chamber" from "Don du Poème," the room where "Hérodiade" took on its elaborations during whole nights. This time we see the room from the outside, through the window, as if in a frame. At the outset, we discover with strangers' eyes the familiar accessories of "Frisson d'Hiver": the frame with its peeling gilt, the old curtains, the empty bed, and the bouquet of roses languishing in a vase.

An incantation arises in this musical, magical darkness. Is it the nurse's voice, or some mysterious echo from the past? She does not even know herself. But the arabesque of the sentence is now immoderately lengthened in motifs that are repeated and more and more interwoven. "I had finally come," wrote Mallarmé, "to a sentence of twenty-two lines, turning on a single verb." This can be traced in the third stanza (lines 38–47), which "turns" on the word "s'élève" (arises) and seems calculated to cast a spell on the reader by enveloping him in "yellow folds of thought" reminiscent of draperies. This voice, an echo of ancient antiphons, alone and like no other,

> À l'heure d'agonie et de luttes funèbres

> (In the hour of death and deathly struggles),

seems vaguely to pierce the silence and the night like a prehistoric star which in reality "never shone." What are these confused traces of a past, these monstrances gone cold from disuse, this pure lacework, these tarnished golds and the old veiled brilliance, if not the last pale vestiges of an ideal that never existed, that was purely potential and now, vanquished and fated, disappears into silence, absorbed in the thickness of the draperies, as the reflection is seen no more in the water of ancient pools?

Thus, time is imperceptibly annulled, "prophetic time," since it announces the twilight of the gods. The old sky burns, twilight is taken for dawn and in the distress of that "last day that is coming to finish everything" the clepsydra runs out, drop by drop. Meanwhile Hérodiade, the cold child abandoned by all, by her father who has left for "Cisalpine lands," even by the angel who no longer accompanies her steps—sensing her body melting like the candle that is slowly consumed by the flame, remains alone:

> *exilée en son coeur précieux*
> *Comme un cygne cachant en sa plume ses yeux,*
> *Comme les mit le vieux cygne en sa plume, allée*
> *De la plume détresse, en l'éternelle allée*
> *De ses espoirs, pour voir les diamants élus*
> *D'une étoile mourante, et qui ne brille plus.*

> (exiled in her precious heart
> Like a swan hiding his eyes in his plumage,
> As the old swan covered them with his feathers, gone
> From the troubled feathers, in the eternal passage
> Of her hopes, to see the chosen diamonds
> Of a star dying, and which shines no more.)

Mallarmé had proclaimed too soon in "l'Azur": "The sky is dead." What had then been a mere phrase was now a reality. A year later, he would recall his "terrible fight with that old and perverse plumage—brought down, fortunately, God! But," he added, "as this struggle took place on his bony wing, which in a death-agony more vigorous than I would have expected of him transported me into the shadows, I fell, victorious—abandonedly and infinitely . . ."

The "Ancient Overture to Hérodiade" unquestionably describes this battle: victory over himself and his old dream, as well as the discovery of Nothingness and despair. "Yes, *I know*, we are merely vain forms of matter." There is no doubt that by this moment Mallarmé had lost all faith. This does not mean, as has been claimed,[4] that he had become a materialist. Rather, "without being acquainted with Buddhism," but through a poetic experience analogous to the mystical experience of the Buddhists, he had discovered a new truth: all is only Maya, illusion, beginning with our own personalities. Wisdom consists of recognizing in the universe a lie "before the Nothing which is the truth." He had touched the depths of night. It would seem that now there remained to him only to sing despairingly of the lie, and to glorify it as both the only testimony and the sublime product of our consciousness and our "invention."

4 E.g., Noulet, *L'oeuvre poétique de Stéphane Mallarmé*, pp. 114 ff.; A. Adam, *Les Lettres* . . . , *op. cit.*, p. 127.

II. Vision of the World

4 · The Spider and His Web

> . . . The center of myself, where I cling like
> a sacred spider to the principal threads already
> spun from my mind.
> LETTER TO AUBANEL, July 28, 1866

I. THE DISCOVERY OF HEGEL

To flee torrid reality I like to evoke cold images: I will tell you
that I have been in the purest glaciers of Esthetics for the last
month—that having found Nothingness, I found the Beautiful—
and that you can't imagine in what lucid altitudes I have been venturing. . . .

So Mallarmé wrote to Cazalis in July, 1866, scarcely four
months after the "nights of Tournon." This unusually enthusiastic tone was due to more than the return of summer.
The *Parnasse contemporain* had begun to appear, and at last
he could read in one of the issues those of his first poems which
he had chosen as his best: "les Fenêtres," "le Sonneur," "À
Celle qui est tranquille" (which later became "Angoisse"),
"Vere Novo" ("Renouveau"), "l'Azur," "les Fleurs," "Soupir,"
"Brise marine," "À un pauvre," and "Épilogue" ("Las de l'amer
repos"). Other than the three or four pieces which had appeared in obscure reviews in 1862, none of his poems had been
published until now. This was then a very exhilarating moment
for the young poet. Yet the slim issue was a keen disappoint-
ment. "I have been the victim of the most regrettable over-
sight, for which I blame Fate and Absence, for I cannot resign
myself without sadness to accusing Mendès of carelessness," he
wrote to Cazalis. Mendès had neglected—or avoided—sending
him the proofs of his text, which consequently lacked his final
corrections. Mallarmé, who already preferred perfection to glory,
felt dishonored: "It was heartbreaking for me, because you

know that I don't care about being published, but in agreeing
to it I insist that the renown brought to me by my work be
based on perfection."

Neither the new season nor the pleasure of seeing himself in
print suffices, then, to explain the total change which some have
called, and not without cause, a veritable conversion. An important discovery must have taken place in the interim. In fact,
the letter of July 16, 1866, to Aubanel confirms this:

> As for me, I have worked harder this summer than in my whole
> life, and I can say that I have worked for my whole life. I have cast
> the foundation for a magnificent work. Each man has his own
> secret. Many die without having found it and will not find it be-
> cause, dead, neither it nor they will any longer exist. I died and
> came back to life with a jewelled key to my last spiritual coffer. Now
> I must open it in the absence of any borrowed impression, and its
> mystery will pour forth across a most beautiful sky. I will need
> twenty years, during which I am going to be cloistered within my-
> self, renouncing all publicity other than reading to my friends.

Guy Delfel maintains that the secret and the discovery were
Platonism. But it is difficult to see what could have led Mallarmé to Plato at that moment. On the other hand, everything
seems to point to the opinion of J. Gengoux and Antoine Adam,
who suppose that the reference is to Hegel's philosophy, to
which Mallarmé was probably introduced through the influence
of Villiers de l'Isle-Adam and, especially, Eugène Lefébure.
Mallarmé's visit to Lefébure in Cannes at the beginning of
April, 1866, during Easter Week, supports this thesis. That stay
was so stimulating and so decisive that two years later he recalled it in these words:

> Decidedly, I am falling from the absolute . . . but the fre-
> quentation of these two years (do you remember? since our stay at
> Cannes) will leave a mark on me that I take as a consecration. I
> am going back into my self, which has been abandoned for two
> years (to Lefébure, May 3, 1868).

Hence it was at Cannes that Mallarmé had "discovered the
Absolute," talking with Lefébure and undoubtedly learning to
know Hegel through him. Cazalis began joking about it the
very next month:

If you become a Buddhist, you understand that everything is lost. Where are we going? Lefébure, an Hegelian; Mallarmé, a Buddhist; Cazalis in Lourcine, Catulle married; what a muddle! It foreshadows the Apocalypse.

Villiers congratulated him in all earnestness in September: "As for Hegel, I am really very happy that you've given some attention to that miraculous genius, that unequaled procreator, that reconstructor of the universe."

It would seem incontestable that not only was Mallarmé undergoing Hegel's influence at that precise moment—an influence which Camille Mauclair insisted upon half a century ago, basing his claim on long conversations with Mallarmé himself—but also that this influence had been in the nature of a revelation.

It has already been pointed out that Mallarmé had lost his faith while pondering "Hérodiade." Through an astonishing effort of lucidity in self searching, he finally dissipated the last traces of the mystical dreams of his childhood and, in so doing, perceived with terror that his individuality itself was mere illusion: a vain form which gradually vanished if merely contemplated in a mirror. At the end of this courageous quest, after all appearances were dissolved, there remained only Nothingness, Emptiness, the "Nothing which is truth." This "crushing thought" left room for nothing but despair.

It was just at this moment that Hegel revealed to Mallarmé that *Nothingness was not an end but a point of departure.* This Nothingness, this Nonbeing, is Being in its first state: a negative state, since it cannot be defined by anything, but containing in itself every possibility, because everything must finally come out of it. In fact, for Hegel the function of universal Life is to elucidate the unknowable mystery of this original state, to reveal it in much the same way that developing fluid reveals the latent image on a photographic plate. The developing agent here is consciousness, the Mind, through which Being is realized, i.e., is affirmed as itself, conforming to its own necessity.

To live is, then, above all else to negate oneself, to become impersonal, to abolish all individuality and empty oneself to nothingness *so that the mystery immanent in the Universe can*

be revealed inwardly in all its purity. One must be the place, the
locale, where the Mind discovers and becomes conscious of itself, as in a mirror. Thus, the more impersonal one has succeeded in becoming, the more faithfully one will reflect the
world, favoring the advent of the Mind, which, by a dialectical
process, should result in Synthesis, become identical with the
very Idea of the universe, and, in so becoming, yield an ex-
haustive explanation of all reality.

At a given moment, Hegel's philosophy furnished Mallarmé
with a confirmation of all his own essential intuitions, as well
as an answer to the questions he had been asking. This was the
crucial moment of his existence. Through a real illumination,
everything was suddenly organized in his mind.

Before going any further, it seems useful to clarify in the light
of his correspondence the essential elements of these ideas,
which would constitute the foundation of his work. Their interpretation has provoked discussion for fifty years.

II. THE FOUNDATIONS OF THE WORK

A. "I died and came back to life." As Guy Delfel has stated
(*L'Esthétique de Stéphane Mallarmé*, p. 49), it was unquestionably a spiritual *conversion*, a change of direction, as the very
images employed by the poet demonstrate: "In *delving so
deeply* in my verse, I have run into . . . Nothingness"; "Having found Nothingness, I found the Beautiful. . . . You can't
imagine in what lucid *altitudes* I have been venturing." To
delve deeply, to be lifted up: here again are the two fundamental and complementary movements that Mallarmé mani-
fested from the beginning.

Guy Delfel claims that there is a cleavage between the two,
between Mallarmé's concept of Nothingness and his concept
of the Beautiful. To be sure, Nothingness was first of all for
him the absolute void, total unconsciousness, the external darkness whence sprang his anguish and despair. But we have seen
that Hegel soon taught him to discover something else in Nothingness. He had suggested the "Spiritual concept of Nothingness" of which Mallarmé spoke several months later, and which
is Being under its still undifferentiated, inexpressible, and mysterious form: zero, pure white, silence. Henceforth, to the poet

who was here interpreting Hegel in his own fashion, Beauty would be included in Nothingness, and he could even affirm that the marvelous lacework he glimpsed "exists already in the bosom of Beauty." His task was to extract it.

B. Mallarmé had found his *secret*. That is, having been freed from his complexes and dreams, having created the void within himself and "in the absence of any borrowed impression," he could penetrate by himself the mystery of that Beauty residing in Nothingness. A letter of 1867 which treats of the experience again will clarify this:

I have just spent a frightening year: my Thought has thought itself through and has arrived at a Divine Concept. All that my being suffered in repercussion during that long death-agony is unspeakable, but fortunately I am perfectly dead, and the most impure region where my Mind can wander is Eternity; my Mind, that solitary inhabitant of its own Purity, which even the reflection of Time no longer obscures. . . . This is to tell you that I am now impersonal and no longer the Stéphane you knew—but an aptitude of the spiritual universe for seeing and developing itself through what I was (to Cazalis, May 14, 1867).

His mind, now impersonal and become the "solitary inhabitant of its own Purity," moves in the Eternal; he has arrived at a Divine Concept, i.e., he is no longer anything but "an aptitude of the spiritual universe for seeing and developing itself" through his own consciousness. Conforming to Hegel's teachings by identifying his mind with the universal Mind, he could thus decipher the mystery of the world in it, as in a mirror. In fact, he continues:

Fragile as my terrestrial apparition is, I can only undergo the developments which are absolutely necessary for the Universe to find its identity in this self of mine. Thus, at the moment of Synthesis, I have just outlined the Work which will be the image of this development. . . .

C. In finding his secret, he found the principle and the justification of his *work*: "There is only Beauty. . . ." So long as he could coincide with the center of the world, the poet would in fact be like a sacred spider spinning his threads, not haphazardly, but according to a plan which of necessity would reproduce the structure of the universe. He explained to Aubanel, who had asked him to shed some light on a few of his more sibylline declarations:

> I have not yet been able to find a minute to clarify the enigmatic aspects of my letter, and I don't like remaining a puzzle to friends such as you. . . . I wanted simply to tell you that I had just laid the foundation for my entire work, after having found the key to myself—the keystone or center, if you will, so as not to mix metaphors—the center of myself where I cling like a sacred spider to the principal threads already spun out of my mind, and with which I will weave at the *meeting places* marvelous laces that I sense, and which already exist in Beauty's bosom (to Aubanel, July 28, 1866).

The great principle was thus discovered: each poem, even each word, like each object it represents, must be a meeting place, a point of encounter. A crossroads in an essential liaison with the rest of the world, it can take on meaning only in its proper place and in its relationship to the All. The networks of metaphors which obsessed Mallarmé thus found their justification as well; each one of them constituted one of those pieces of lace that the poet was unconsciously weaving in the image of immanent Beauty. Henceforth, they must merely be purified of all personal intrusion; the poems must be no longer "intuitions revealing [his] temperament" but, in some way, soundings in Beauty's depths.

D. Thanks to Hegel, Mallarmé could now also justify his theory of the poetic "mystery," formulated at twenty. For mystery is not, properly speaking, the unknowable, but only what is hidden from the layman who is still blinded by his individuality. In other words, it is the beauty of the spiritual universe as revealed to pure Consciousness. These are undoubtedly the ideas Mallarmé confided in some unfortunately lost letters to Lefébure, if one can judge by the latter's rather skeptical answers:

> I have sufficiently grasped your poetic theory of Mystery, which is very true and confirmed by history. Up to the present, every time man has glimpsed the true, i.e., *the logical constitution of the Universe,* he has thrown himself back in horror toward infinite illusion. . . . But I fear that men will quickly lose the habit of proposing riddles *to which they have the key* (May 27, 1867. Italics mine).

And several days later:

That is the idea which must have led you to reject from your work all the ligaments that tie Beauty to the grosser part of man, and the heaviness of matter. You have cut the earth-laden roots of your flowers. . . . You find yourself at a unique moment where it is impossible for you to condense the quintessence of the Beautiful. The flower whose root you nourished keeps its sap when cut, and loses its earthy footing. . . . You are at the supreme point after which there is nothing left but descent. It is to be feared (and unfortunately to be believed) that the Science of Mystery and the analysis of the Divine degrade poetry and topple religion, cutting through the history of humanity on earth and leaving an ever-open wound (June 2, 1867).

For Mallarmé there really was a "Science of Mystery" and an "analysis of the Divine," since he was convinced that the logical structure of the universe where Beauty resides can be penetrated by intuition. But in order to attain this, *mystery must be preserved* in all its purity. Therefore it is necessary to "cut the roots" of poetry, its attachment to earth and coarse life, at the risk of losing one's footing. Mallarmé was at least forewarned of the danger stalking him.

E. Furthermore, that logical constitution of the universe left no place to chance. It was founded on a *necessity* to which every authentic poem must conform. "There is only Beauty; and only one perfect expression of it: Poetry." Therefore, everything must be foreseen. There exists only one Work worthy of the name. Having reached the "hour of Synthesis"—a very Hegelian expression—Mallarmé fixed the entire structure of his Work. He already perceived its "general delineation" and was sketching the architectural blueprint. Renouncing all haste, all desire for publication, with an abnegation that can be found elsewhere only in his disciple Valéry, he gave himself twenty years to write it:

. . . I foresee that I shall need twenty years for the five books which will compose the Work, and . . . I shall wait, reading fragments only to friends like you—and scoffing at glory as at a worn-out trifle. What is relative immortality, and frequent passage through the minds of imbeciles, next to the joy of contemplating Eternity and enjoying it, living, in oneself (to Aubanel, July 28, 1866)?

F. Poetic experience or metaphysical quest? "Until 1869," writes Antoine Adam, "Mallarmé wanted to translate an experience, not construct a metaphysics." The expression "enjoy Eternity in oneself" would seem to prove this, if one forgot that "there is only real knowledge insofar as it implies identification of subject and object, or, if it is preferable to consider the relationship inversely, an assimilation of the object by the subject" (R. Guénon: *Les états multiples de l'Ête*, p. 109). Metaphysics was no more a gratuitous speculation for Mallarmé than it is for Oriental thinkers. It was a lived experience, and only through a true participation in the mystery of the universe could the poet render a valid translation of it. Poetry was to be from this moment on the means by which Mallarmé would not only enjoy Eternity but also realize himself in the eternal, according to his own necessity.

III. GLORIFICATION OF BEAUTY

In 1866, Mallarmé had only a glimpse of what the projected Work would be. But he already dreamed of attempting an expression of his new ideas in a poetic form:

I am in the process of laying the foundations of a book on the Beautiful. My mind is *moving in the Eternal*. . . . I am taking a rest with the assistance of three short poems which will be unprecedented, all three to the glorification of Beauty (to Catulle Mendès).

There is good reason to believe that the three short poems alluded to here are the first draft, now lost, of three sonnets presented together twenty years later, in 1887, to the *Revue Indépendante*: "Tout orgueil fume-t-il du soir" (All pride smokes in the evening); "Surgi de la croupe et du bond" (Sprung up from the croup and the leap); "Une dentelle s'abolit" (A piece of lace is abolished). As has already been pointed out, they evoke not only the familiar décor of those nights of 1865–66 and of "Don du Poème": the room, the fireplace, the ceiling, the lamp. They also incorporate certain themes of "Sainte," such as that of the mandola, and especially of "l'Ouverture ancienne d'Hérodiade," such as the lacework of the bed, the vase of flowers, and the obsessive words, abandon, death-agony, sepulcher, shadows. But, as Mallarmé said, they

are still clearly a "glorification of Beauty." Although the vocabulary attests to their conception at this time, the *tone* of the
poems is quite new. They are poems of absence, to be sure, but
of a promising absence that instead of being a pure nothingness
is a "creux néant musicien" (a hollow music-making nothingness) where all Beauty resides in potential. In writing these
poems, Mallarmé's mind was truly moving in the Eternal and
putting his latest discoveries to the test. In the very terms of
Hegel's intent, having created the void within himself, he was
receiving impressions of what surrounded him, while attempting
to "expel everything that could give a specific content to the
object," and, through the vanishing of the object, to bring forth
the Idea from his being.

The parallelism of the three sonnets is striking. All three take
their point of departure from the sight of a familiar object
chosen from the poet's own room: a console, a chandelier,
a curtain framing a window. But all three objects are merely
pretexts. Through a true intervention of the "demon of analogy," each one *suggests* another image: the console which supports a marble plaque evokes a fireplace, as the chandelier with
its curved contours evokes a vase and the curtain a bedstead.
Three appearances dreamed by the poet—each of which by the
very fact that it is only an appearance attesting to the *absence*
of something: there could no more be a fire in the false fireplace
than there could be a rose in the seeming vase or a bed in the
sham bedstead.

But is that not precisely what creates Beauty? A console, a
chandelier, a curtain, considered as objects cannot claim any
esthetic quality. They exist, nothing more. Their value arises
from the analogy they present with other objects likely to endow
them with meaning: the sense of an absence, but also of a need,
an expectation of something. Such is the actual poetic "impression" from which Mallarmé began writing: a console, its marble
seemingly waiting for the red glow of the fire; a chandelier with
a curved neck, seeming to want to offer a rose; lacework which
unfolds on the promise of a bed. The fire, the rose, the bed:
obsessive absences which succeed after much consideration in
eliciting in us the *idea* of what should be—not merely a fire, a
rose, a bed, but Fire, Rose, Bed.

There is more. These objects evoke more than just the appearances of other objects. As in "Hérodiade" or "l'Ouverture ancienne," they call forth a whole inner world of human feelings and states of mind, generally through the coupling of a new analogy with an object or a being that will serve as an intercessor. Thus the console, illuminated by a reflection of the setting sun, suggests a torch, which in the poet's soul gives rise in turn to the idea of pride, a vacillating fire which is already nothing more than smoke. The chandelier's supple forms suggest both the image of an empty cup and that of a sylph, which in their turn awaken the idea of a chimera, the ever-elusive dream that is always different, even to two lovers. Finally, the curtain suggests at once the absence of a bed and a birth, a woman's womb, a mandola, a hollow nothingness where the poet's golden dreams lie dormant, ready to be born.

A literal interpretation of these three poems would be difficult to propose here because all were visibly reworked before reaching their final state, the only one extant today. Mallarmé introduced too many new procedures in them, most of which date from after 1866 and are of a complexity that is apparently still disconcerting. Let it suffice for the time being to show that these pieces, while having their roots in the intimate experience of the Tournon years, are at the same time projections toward the future. The triptych constitutes a kind of little three-act play in which the poet's inner drama is presented in striking condensation.

The first sonnet [1] is very exactly located in the same room as "Don du Poème," but projected into the past like the one in "l'Ouverture ancienne" and embellished with "maint riche mais chu trophée" (many a rich but fallen trophy). "L'hoir" (the heir), the inheritor of the race, i.e., the poet, is absent. But his anxieties are still there, represented by the two arms of the console which seem—a new analogy—to grip the heavy marble as if it were a coffin. And in the cold abandon of an evening full of "affres nécessaires" (necessary pangs), slowly his pride is exhaled and dissipated into smoke, the pride of an individuality that was only an illusion, like the fire of the absent hearth.

1 Commentary: Thibaudet, p. 230. Noulet, p. 437. Mauron, p. 186; II, p. 151. Soula, p. 67. Gengoux, p. 182.

In the second sonnet,[2] evening has given way to the darkness of night. All the poet's bitter nocturnal vigils are there, but now without any lamp to illuminate his work. It is the agony of this flowerless vase, this empty goblet, this lamp with its "interrupted" and expectant throat, the glasswork and its ephemeral appearances—a scroll curving now like a croup, now like a leap—evoking the form of a sylph, the impalpable genius of the air. The vase is irremediably empty, "pur d'aucun breuvage" (innocent of any beverage) other than its very "veuvage" (widowhood), the inexhaustible nothingness it contains: those who gave birth to the sylph were not able to drink from it, able to quench their thirst only with the vain chimeras of love or dreams. By contrast, the sylph, like the interrupted glasswork, seems in a naïve kiss to drink some absence of rose directly from the darkness. Here the poet "discovers Nothingness," but still without knowing that it encloses Beauty.

Finally, the third element of the triptych[3] brings us, as in "l'Ouverture," to the first glimmer of dawn: a vague whiteness and pallid windowpanes, against which a bit of lacework clings and "s'enfuit" (flees). It seems artificial and unreal in the doubtful and final play of night slowly dying before the dawning day. Yet it is as if this double curtain, which partially and so indiscreetly opens on Nothingness—Oh, blasphemy!—were still struggling in a last combat with itself. Is this the death of every dream? No, because the lace floats impalpably at the border of Nothingness. But the poet, he who "du rêve se dore" (gilds himself with the dream), with that dream that he knows does not exist ("ce Rêve qu'il sait n'être pas," as he once wrote

2 Commentary: Noulet, p. 438. Mauron, p. 190. Soula, p. 77. Gengoux, p. 187. The interpretation of this sonnet has been the object of much controversy. Most commentators follow the opinion of T. Wyzewa, who sees it merely as a flowerless vase. Not incorrectly, Mauron recognized a lamp that will not light and Gengoux, an empty goblet. Each made the mistake of eliminating or neglecting the other interpretations, for, as we have seen, only the *combination* of the three interpretations permits the alignment of each sonnet with its "neighbor" to give it meaning. Why did Mauron not pursue his hypothesis to the end? He would have understood that the enigmatic sylph was not "painted on the ceiling," as he said, but suggested analogically to Mallarmé by the very form of the chandelier.

3 Commentary: Noulet, p. 441; II, p. 100. Mauron, p. 192. Soula, p. 85. Gengoux, p. 191.

to Cazalis), *knows* now that the "hollow nothingness" contains
Beauty in its bosom. That bosom is the ineffable musician, the
mandola which, somnolent in the poet's soul, encloses in its
womb the Poem in its potential state: the Work, his offspring,
ready to see the light of day and to spring "toward some window"—beyond the room and the world of men.

These are truly unprecedented poems, rendering a sound
previously unheard of, with their superimposed harmonies and
their arabesques entwining over a void that encloses every
possibility. They are the "glorification of Beauty," if it is true
that Beauty, as Mallarmé was to believe henceforth, is beyond
any real object, a world of ideas that is far from possessing the
immortal reality of the Platonic sky, but which is nevertheless
the "sky of fixity," the necessary abode of eternal forms.

If these are the sonnets mentioned in the letter to Mendès
and they were really written at this date, it is possible to believe
that Cazalis was aware of them when, a little later, he offered
Mallarmé this homage, so rare from one poet to another:

My friend, I wept reading your letter, wept not to see you dead,
since your death made you climb back to life, into the tranquil sky
you had dreamed of entering, but wept with respect and admiration. You are the greatest poet of your time, Stéphane, know it; and
elevated as you may be, may this homage, my poor friend whose
life has been so sorrowful, so holy, so sad, may this homage console what human remains are left in you. All of us are nothing next
to you. We are children who can hardly stammer, whose poetry
has not yet been born and perhaps will never be born. No one has
meditated and suffered more than you; no other has gone further
into the abyss; you see then that you are the greatest, the only great
one among us. Finish your work. I ask it of destiny, and I plead
for it with all my soul.

5 · The Sorcerer's Book

> When the breath of his ancestors tries to blow
> out the candle (thanks to which, perhaps, the
> letters of the sorcerer's book still exist), he says,
> "Not yet!"
>
> "IGITUR," EARLY STUDY

I. FIRST GLANCES AT OCCULTISM

From the age of twenty, when in "l'Art pour tous" he first spoke of the golden clasps on old missals and inviolate hieroglyphics, Mallarmé, as we have seen, had dreamed of inventing an entirely new poetry, an immaculate language of hieratic and mysterious formulae. From that time on, it can almost be said that each one of his poems could be viewed as an endeavor in that direction: "It is rather a new genre, this poetry," he wrote to Cazalis about "Renouveau." He often spent several days balancing its parts beforehand so that the whole would be harmonious and as close as possible to the Beautiful. Of "l'Azur" he wrote: "I swear to you that there is not one word of it that did not cost me several hours of search."

Soon afterward he attacked "Hérodiade," "in terror, for I am inventing a language which must necessarily spring from a very new poetics." A poetics of the effect produced, in which words must retreat before the intention and be charged with mystery:

If you knew how many desperate nights and dream-filled days must be sacrificed to succeed in making verses original (which I have never done until now) and worthy in their supreme mysteries of rejoicing a poet's soul! What a study of the sound and color of words, of music and painting, must be absorbed by your thought, however beautiful it may be, in order to be poetic (to Cazalis, July, 1865)!

63

One night, thanks to a long meditation, "Hérodiade" suddenly became the Poem, the Work, with capital letters: "I was fortunate enough last night to see my Poem in its nudity, and I mean to attempt the Work this evening." However, this was nothing yet. After the Easter stay in Cannes in 1866 and the discovery of Hegel, Mallarmé was still bent over "Hérodiade," for which he claimed to have found at last "le fin mot," the perfect word. At the same time, however, he was casting "the foundations of a book about the Beautiful," and then "the foundations of a magnificent work." A work? No; shortly after, he clarified: *his* work, "the entire Work," for which he was then establishing the outline: five books, which it would take him twenty years to write.

From this moment on, he had taken his position. For twenty years he worked in the shadows, cloistered within himself, spinning his web and elaborating what he would soon be calling "the Great Work, as our ancestors the alchemists used to say." For there was only one Book to create, one which would reflect the structure and development of the universe and which would explain its hidden meaning through this reflection. Neither his conviction nor the terms in which he expressed it had changed in 1885 when he wrote in his *Autobiography*, addressed to Verlaine:

It has been twenty years now, and in spite of the loss of so many hours I believe, with sadness, that I acted wisely [in making sure of a livelihood by teaching]. For, leaving aside bits of prose, the verses of my youth, and the echoes which followed them, published more or less everywhere each time the first issues of a Literary Review appeared, I always dreamed of and attempted something else, with an alchemist's patience, prepared to sacrifice all vanity and satisfaction to it, as they used to burn their furniture and roofbeams to feed the furnace for the Great Work. What is it? It is difficult to say: a book, quite simply, in many volumes, a book which would be a book, architectural and premeditated, and not a collection of chance inspirations, however marvelous they might be... I will go even further, I will say: the Book, convinced that basically there is only one, attempted unknowingly by whoever has written, even Geniuses. The orphic explanation of the Earth, which is the poet's sole duty and the literary game par excellence . . .

It has been clearly established by now that if Mallarmé compared himself to an alchemist and his work to the Great

Work, it was not merely a literary manner of speaking. Certainly, he does not seem to have participated in an initiation rite any more than he threw himself into occult experiments in matter. But it is known that for the Cabala, as for all secret traditions, there are multitudinous ways of initiation as well as means of acting on the world for the initiated. Among these, language is clearly a privileged means, and one might say even the very best, if one accepts language as the distant heir of the Word, endowed in ancient times with a truly magical power. Mallarmé was then within his rights when he considered himself the heir of the alchemists, inasmuch as he was a poet.

Besides, the influence of more than one master or friend would have sufficed to turn his curiosity toward occultism. Nothing proves that Mallarmé was really acquainted with the work of Nerval, but we know what importance Baudelaire attached to Swedenborg, Fourier, Lavater, and all of their predecessors who were concerned with correspondences and the "universal analogy," from Plato and Plotinus to Jacob Boehme and Paracelsus. Even more recently, Villiers de l'Isle-Adam had been nourished by these ideas, to which, moreover, Hegel was no stranger. As for Lefébure, although the allusions in his letters to Mallarmé are not very explicit, his research into antiquity as well as his personal tastes had undoubtedly initiated him to some extent into the secret traditions of Greece and, more especially, Egypt.

So it is not inconceivable that Mallarmé was first initiated into the rudiments of occultism under the direct influence of Lefébure, as he was initiated into Hegel. In any case, before Easter of 1866 there is no formal trace of it in his work, and we have seen that it is unnecessary to have any such notion, as did Denis Saurat, in order to elucidate "Hérodiade" or "Don du Poème." During the summer of 1866, in the same letter in which Villiers congratulated Mallarmé on his discovery of Hegel, he said:

When will the *Traité des pierres précieuses* [Treatise on Precious Stones] appear? I have more confidence in your alchemy than in that of Auriolus Theophrastus Bombastis, called the divine Paracelsus. Nevertheless, I bring to your attention the *Dogmes et Rituel de Haute Magie* [Dogma and Ritual of High Magic] of Eliphas Lévy ... if it can be found in your town library. It is astonishing.

There is no doubt that Mallarmé was then paying serious attention to the alchemy mentioned by Villiers, for he was contemplating a *Traité des pierres précieuses* which he never did finish, if he even began it. According to J. Scherer's likely hypothesis, he planned for it to contain both his meditations on pure words—which he began in that period to compare to jewels—and a symbolism probably inspired by Villiers. It is a known fact that for an occultist each precious stone possesses a symbolic meaning and even a magical influence, and that the alchemists' image-laden vocabulary made great use of this. These meditations on precious stones certainly drew Mallarmé's attention to the value and importance not only of the word in general, but also of the *name* and its properly magic power over souls.

Even more, they must have helped him to become aware of his poetic intuitions. The presence of that demon of analogy which had so early haunted him and led him to endow metaphor with a quasi-metaphysical importance was now inscribed in the very structure of the universe. From earliest times, every more or less occult tradition has affirmed the unity of all creation and the dependence of its structure on the principle of analogy between the macrocosm and the microcosm. Thus, as Baudelaire, following Swedenborg, had already said in his article on Victor Hugo, "the sky is a very great man," and

everything—form, movement, number, color, perfume, in the *spiritual* as well as the *natural* is meaningful, reciprocal, converse, *corresponding*. . . . Everything is hieroglyphics, and we know that symbols are obscure only in a relative manner, i.e., depending on the purity, the goodwill, or the native clairvoyance of souls.

When these lines appeared in 1862, Mallarmé had doubtless seen them only as a suggestion and a pretext for *inventing* a hieroglyphic language for poetry. Now they were clarified for him: *Poetry is not invented, it is discovered.* As Baudelaire put it, "What is a poet, if not a translator, a decipherer?"

Since then, as Mallarmé confided much later to Claudel, the poet's task has been to wonder, at each object presented, "What does that mean?" But for the true poet the discovery of the meaning does not suffice. As Baudelaire states, he must also impose it on the reader through a truly "suggestive magic"; he must recreate and bring forth the Idea of the object, a living reality, through the simple power of words, like the magician. The "Overture to Hérodiade" had spoken of the "magical shade with symbolic charms." Thus, from the shadows of the unconscious, the poet's consciousness will bring forth a world, or, better, bring the world back to life; not the world of material objects lost in the infinite multiplicity of appearances, but that world of ideas and pure concepts where objects are symbols. (Let us not attach too much importance to that word. Mallarmé seems scarcely to have noticed it at this time, despite the "forests of symbols" in Baudelaire's sonnet. The use of the adjective, "symbolic," in a line of "l'Ouverture" is surely a kind of anticipatory intuition. As for the prestigious name, "symbol," destined for such a future, it would be, strangely enough, many long years before it appeared in his work.)

II. THE SONNET IN -yx

Mallarmé was dreaming now of being a magician of language. He did not yet quite know how to go about it. Yet in a letter he spoke of his "cabalistic predilections" for the number three, "that supreme digit"; and he had certainly learned from his masters in occultism that each sound had originally possessed a special power of incantation. Perhaps too, as Scherer thinks, he had read in the *Note sur la philologie appliquée* (Note on Applied Philology) published in 1865 by Émile Chasles, also a professor of English and part-time linguist, the passage discussing the special properties and particular affinities of the letters of the alphabet and the elementary sounds, which had lost their primitive purity through the ages. Mallarmé thought that the poet's privilege and function was precisely to restore this purity. But paradoxically, two years after having "discovered the Beautiful," he had written nothing, except, no doubt, for the three sonnets in glorification of Beauty. Was he afraid of tarnishing the purity of the perfect work of his dreams by beginning to write it? Or was this impasse the revenge of the demon of impotency?

His apparent "conversion" had not conjured away the crisis he had been involved in since 1865. As has been seen, his con-

victions remained founded on despair in the most precise sense
of the word, i.e., the loss of all hope of a personal afterlife. It
had been a permanent loss, confirmed by many a later statement, such as this: "It would not be without a really heartrending grief that I would enter the supreme Disappearance, if
I had not finished my work." He needed several years to attain
a relative serenity. Up until 1870, each winter brought on a new
crisis accompanied by growing disorders in his physical and
mental health.

His transfer to Besançon in October, 1866, plunged him into
profound distress. In spite of Lefébure's affectionate and encouraging letters, and despite such budding new friendships
as that with Verlaine, who sent him his *Poèmes Saturniens,* he
was once more discouraged outside of his familiar room. "Ah!
the old mirror of Silence is broken!" This did not prevent him
from pursuing fertile, if painful, meditations. "I have just spent
a frightening year," he wrote to Cazalis, in the already quoted
letter of May 14, 1867.

In October, 1867, after much effort, he finally arrived in
Avignon, the land of his dreams. There at least, in that "adora-
ble climate" among his friends of the Félibrige, a society of
Provençal writers, he hoped to recover his equilibrium. But
hardly had he settled down than a luckless lung congestion
condemned him to bed for many weeks. "The entire edifice of
my physical and moral health, so patiently reconstructed, has
broken down; useless, this lengthy insect's labor. I am beginning
all over again" (to Cazalis, January 27, 1868). New efforts, new
anxieties, but also new meditations. He wrote to Lefébure: "I
spend moments bordering on madness glimpsed between
ecstasies that restore my balance. I am in a state of crisis that
cannot go on" (May 3, 1868). To Coppée: "Having come to
a horrible vision of a pure work, I have almost lost my reason
and the meanings of the most common words."

For him to return to poetry it was necessary for Cazalis to
ask him for a sonnet to include in an anthology. Even then
Mallarmé took pains to point out that he would not touch the
Work, "so well prepared and stratified, representing, as it can,
the universe," that he could not lift anything out of it, i.e.,
write anything that would be a detached fragment. Moreover,

he had just admitted to Lefébure that he was "coming back down from the absolute," adding: "After all, poems that are only tinged with the absolute are already beautiful, and there are few of them."

In response to his friend's wish, he took up an old project, an extract "from a projected study of the word." In other words, it was a poem "only tinged with the absolute": an exercise in virtuosity, a kind of experiment in poetic language, nonetheless meaningful because it would propose the rediscovery of certain powers of language. In sending the sonnet to Cazalis, he warned him of its very particular nature: "It is inverted. . . . I mean that its meaning, if there is one (but I could resign myself to the contrary, thanks to the dose of poetry it encloses, it seems to me), is evoked by an internal mirage of the words themselves. By allowing oneself to murmur it several times, one experiences a rather cabalistic sensation" (July, 1868).

The original text [1] of this piece has been found, and it is quite different from the one that Mallarmé later gave for the 1887 edition. One must refer to the 1868 version to understand its genesis and original meaning.

Mallarmé clarified for Cazalis the décor and initial perception which gave birth to the sonnet. A room, "unfurnished except for the suggested presence of some vague console . . . a nocturnally open window"; and, in the back of the room, a mirror hanging in a "bellicose and dying frame." Once again, we find the familiar accessories of the nights of Tournon and Avignon: Hérodiade's mirror, the console, and the window from the sonnets on Beauty. There is also an analogous *impression:* "A night made of absence and questioning," comments Mallarmé; a "décor of absence," says the first version. A multiple absence, as it were, an absence of the evening *abolished* by night (as the lacework—and the dawn in "l'Ouverture"— were abolished by the day), an absence in the mirror of the god promised by its enclosure, an absence of the object on the console, an absence, finally, of the Master. If Mallarmé speaks

1 Cf. *Oeuvres complètes*, p. 1482. The commentaries bear on the 1887 text: Noulet, p. 453; Mauron, p. 162; Soula, p. 137; Gengoux, p. 53; E. Souriau, *Correspondance des Arts*, p. 251; Michaud, *Message* . . . , p. 184.

of a "room with someone inside," that someone has left to delve
into the waters of the Styx, and everything takes place as if he
were dead—therefore, absent from the room.

What is this Master? A poet dead in 1866, as Mauron sup-
poses? But the original title of the piece, "Sonnet allégorique
de lui-même" (Allegorical Sonnet of Himself) proves, as most
of its commentators have seen, that it simply concerns Mallarmé, who has "become impersonal" and departed for the land
of oblivion "avec tous ses objets dont le réve s'honore" (with
all his objects by which the dream is honored), i.e., with his
old dreams, his "rich but fallen trophies," and his angels. Here
the metaphorical meaning of the piece emerges. As in "Tout
orgueil fume-t-il du soir," the empty room is the poet's very
soul. The vague golden reflections which alone still animate it
are the death-throes of his dreams. It is night—the definitive
version will say, "this midnight"—and now the Master has
created the absolute void, Nothingness, within himself. Not the
slightest fold, not the slightest impurity remains in his soul,
just as there is no longer any "ptyx" on the console.

This "ptyx" has excited a great deal of discussion. What
meaning should be given to this mysterious word? Should one
believe Mallarmé, who asked Lefébure to send him its real
meaning while he was meditating on the sonnet that he proposed to write? He added, "I have been assured that it does
not exist in any language, which I prefer by far so as to have
the pleasure of creating it through the magic of rhyme." It
has been tempting to hold to this interpretation, as I have done
myself, and to see the word as the acme of nothingness, represented by a word devoid of meaning. But Lefébure must have
put his erudition to work for the poet. Thanks to him and to
Greek etymology, it can hardly be doubted that Mallarmé
eventually understood the ptyx to be one of those curving
shells which used to ornament old-fashioned fireplaces, and in
which one can hear the sound of the sea. As the word can also
indicate a fold or pleat, its ambiguity is assured; and, as E.
Fraenkel has ingeniously noted (*Perspectives sur Mallarmé*),
the absence of the ptyx suggests at the same time the total
emptiness of the lodging and the total purity of the soul.

Yet on the total vacuity inscribed in the very frame of the

mirror, "en l'obscurcissement de la glace" (in the darkening of the glass),[2] an image emerges. It is not a reality, but a reflection, "the stellar and incomprehensible reflection of the Great Bear," says Mallarmé, "de scintillation le septuor" (the septet of scintillation). It is as if the poet, having vanished into the mirror, is already nothing more than an "aptitude of the spiritual universe" for seeing itself through him.

But who ever claimed that irreducible mystery does not exist? Once all is abolished in the depths of absolute absence, at the extremities of the empty sky discovered by Mallarmé, something *incomprehensible* subsists: the luminous trace on a black background of a gigantic roll of the dice, a constellation of which we can perceive only a pale reflection on the mirror of our souls, and which is the very symbol of Beauty.

There is a cabalistic overtone to these seven luminous points on the mirror. The number seven is surrounded with prestige in all symbolic speculations, and magic attaches much importance to mirrors. But in addition to this, Mallarmé wants to capture us through the magic of sounds as well as through the magic of the mirror, with a subtle interplay of echoes and reflections.

The night's onyx, the dying frame's gold and the Great Bear's seven points scattered among the fourteen lines alternately light up and go out. The "i's" and the sibilant consonants scintillate, too, in every corner of the sonnet. The two lone sonorities "or" and "yx" dance, especially in the rhyme, like incomprehensible fires. It could be called a mental game, a tour de force worthy of the fifteenth-century Rhetoricians, not only to choose the rarest rhyme, *-yx*, for a sonnet, but also to make sure of using its feminine equivalent in the tercets. But from this the game derives all its meaning; for this chamber with its innumerable mirrors is the symbol of the world, containing in its depths, disquieting and haunting, an irreducible unknown, the X.

---

2 Chassé, convinced not incorrectly that Mallarmé often referred to Littré's etymologies, sees the "oubli fermé par le cadre" (oblivion enclosed by the frame) of the later version as meaning "the contours of lividness arrested by the frame" (*obliviscor*, from *lividus*). But it is obvious that one meaning does not exclude the other.

III. "IGITUR"

The mysterious "Sonnet in -yx" constitutes then for Mallarmé not a detached fragment of the Work, but a world apart, a closed and self-sufficient microcosm, at once the reflection, the witness, and the symbol of the poet. Yet Mallarmé had not despaired of undertaking the Great Work of which he had been speaking to his friends for two years. He seemed to have defined it in May, 1867: "Three poems in verse, of which 'Hérodiade' is the overture . . . and four poems in prose, on the spiritual concept of Nothingness" (to Cazalis). He was apparently still working on the four prose poems during the summer of 1869 while visiting Lecques, whence he wrote Cazalis:

> It is a tale by which I want to fell the old monster of Impotency, its subject, by the way, so that I may cloister myself in my great labor, already restudied. If the tale is done, I am cured; *Similia similibus.*

This tale was no longer an integral part of the Work, then. It would constitute only an introduction, a sort of psychoanalysis. The poet would apply to himself in the psychotherapeutic domain the methods dear to homeopathy, *similia similibus*—describing one's sickness in order to be cured of it. In fact, since 1866 his ailment had only aggravated, despite his courageous efforts to thwart it. The prolonging of his exercise in "depersonalization" was asking too much of his strength. Neurasthenia stalked him. He was sometimes unable to write: "The simple act of writing brings hysteria to my head." In February, 1869, he had to dictate to his wife his letters to his friends. Still lucid, however, he defined his experiment:

> My brain, invaded by the Dream, rejecting its external functions, which no longer made claims on it, was on the point of perishing in permanent insomnia; I prayed fervently to the Great Night, which heard me and spread out its darkness. The first phase of my life was finished. Consciousness, worn out with shadows, is slowly awakening, forming a new man, and must find my Dream again after the creation of the latter. This will take several years, during which I have to relive humanity's life from the time of its infancy and its first self-awareness (to Cazalis, February 19, 1869).

The spiritual death of the poet is precisely the subject of "Igitur," a strange, hermetic work which Mallarmé read one year later in his study at Avignon to his friends Catulle Mendès and Villiers de l'Isle-Adam. They had just returned from Munich, where they had visited Wagner. Villiers was enthusiastic, but Mendès, stupefied, stamped his foot with impatience and made no attempt to hide his disapproval. This reaction may have moved Mallarmé to judge his work severely in later times. In any case, he never published it.

Yet it is one of his most important works: "Igitur, ou la Folie d'Elbehnon" (Igitur, or Elbehnon's Madness), the last word taken from the Hebrew, according to Rolland de Renéville. The title is presumably the first word of Genesis II: "Igitur perfecti sunt coeli et terra et omnis ornatus eorum," if it is true that, as Renéville asserts, "this sentence refers to the angels, the Elohim, creative powers emanating from Jehovah, in short, all the stars," and if "El behnon in Hebrew means the son of the Elohim." Igitur is, then, the son of the stars who have created heaven and earth "sur le mode principiel" (in the primordial mode), before any other manifestation. He is at the same time the spiritual brother, the echo, the reflection of unmanifested creation. "Therefore": Igitur is the consequence, the logical and necessary product in the human order, of the creative principle from which everything came. He is the anonymous and impersonal archetype, the hero of a tale in which nothing happens.

But he is above all the poet himself, obsessed by the "old monster of Impotency." Even at the time of "Renouveau," impotency for Mallarmé brought boredom with it. Or rather, it *was* boredom: "L'impuissance s'étire en un long bâillement" (Impotency stretches out in a long yawn). Only then it was a sort of physical sensation, a heaviness of the whole being, a strange numbness that took hold of the poet when he had concentrated too long on his ideal, the white page, or the blue, and felt suddenly discouraged by their demands. At the present moment, he was trying to discover the profound reasons for this impotency. He had the feeling that the cause was metaphysical and inherent to his human condition. So he attempted to give an account of his life in Chapter III of "Igitur":

"Névrose, ennui (ou Absolu!)" (Neurosis, ennui [or Absolute!])—for him they are all one. His neurosis was his obsessive fixation on the Absolute, symbolized by the white page, an obsession always translated by the feeling of impotency. What had he been seeking in his long nocturnal meditations? "I have always lived with my soul fixed on the clock." Why? In the hope of immobilizing time, of arresting its inexorable flight, of being able to grasp, once, "the absolute present of things," in the same way that the blank page is the presence of space in its purest form, absolute presence. But at the time of "Hérodiade" and "l'Ouverture ancienne" he thought he was achieving this by simply closing the curtains and continuously making them thicker so as not to lose the least atom of time.

Then his "Idea was completed," i.e., he discovered Hegel, and "after having found Nothingness, found the Beautiful." He understood that what prevented him from grasping the absolute was a "malady of ideality," an old dream that would not die in him, the "whole past of his race." This long atavism of faith and hope in a problematic immortality made him desperately seek his image in the mirror and try to retain time in the draperies. Wanting to secure both at any price, he then turned them into pure ennui. Why could he not consent to see his image effaced in the mirror, to let the last particles of time escape through the trembling curtains, and break down boredom once and for all into its primary elements? When he finally understood the necessity of doing this, he attempted to withdraw from time. He underwent the test of the mirror, fixing one's image until it disappears in "an awful sensation of eternity," and he found himself again, impersonal, in his empty room, amidst the rigid, dead furniture.

This is where the real tale of "Igitur" begins. Its first chapter opens with a prose answer to the "Sonnet in -yx":

Certainement subsiste une présence de Minuit. L'heure n'a pas disparu par un miroir, ne s'est pas enfouie en tentures, évoquant un ameublement par sa vacante sonorité. Je me rappelle que son or allait feindre en l'absence un joyau nul de rêverie, riche et inutile survivance, sinon que sur la complexité marine et stellaire d'une orfèvrerie se lisait le hasard infini des conjonctions.

(Certainly a presence of Midnight endures. The hour has not yet disappeared through a mirror, has not buried itself in the draperies, evoking furnishings with its empty sonority. I remember that its gold was going to feign, in the absence, a null jewel of reverie, a rich and useless survival, except that, on the marine and stellar complexity of a work of gold, there could be read the infinite fortuitousness of conjunctions.)

Only, from one to the other there is a complete reversal. One has the impression of a discovery: negation is followed by triumphant affirmation: "Certainly a presence of Midnight endures." Igitur's image had only *seemed* to disappear in the glass, time had only seemed to escape him and "bury itself." But at the precise moment when the hero was totally forgetting himself, dying to himself and his race, to his entire past, he was suddenly "projected outside of time." Something like a fall occurred, "the fall of the hour," as if the gates of the tomb were closing upon him. By the very virtue of oblivion, time was dissolved, "resolved." Everything was fixed in an eternal attitude, and he himself was immobilized "in a long-dreamed narcotic calm of pure self."

Then, in this unique and unified hour, the great scission is brought about: the creative act par excellence, that of the First Day when light was separated from darkness—in metaphysical language, the Infinite from the Potential, or essence from substance.[3]

De l'Infini se séparent et les constellations et la mer demeurées, en l'extériorité, de réciproques néants, pour en laisser l'essence, à l'heure unie, faire le présent absolu des choses.

(From the Infinite the constellations and the sea [= the primeval waters] are separated, remaining, externally [= in external darkness], reciprocal nothingnesses [= substance, universal Potentiality], leaving their essence to make the absolute present of things at the unified hour.)

And by the same token, a vague light emerges in the room where everything else is relegated to shadow: the host's

3 Cf. R. Guénon: *Les états multiples de l'Être*, pp. 21–22, for these correspondences.

face, illuminated by mystery. Its gleam is reflected and summed up in the pallor of a book opened on the table.[4]

In this hieratic scene, the poet is ready to reproduce the original act of Creation through a veritable ascesis. Having attained total purity, he contains within himself the mystery which is also the true light: the essence of all things. Opposite him, the open, white, and vacant book waits in the shadow like the primeval waters for the Spirit to come and fecundate it.

Yet the moment has not yet come—if one can speak in this way of intemporal states—to make the creative gesture. For Mallarmé/Igitur must first of all "relive humanity's life from the time of its infancy and its first self-awareness," as he wrote Cazalis. But what is happening? Despite the total fall of time, everything has not fallen into silence. Mallarmé still notices "une douteuse perception de pendule" (a dubious perception of a pendulum) which seems to be expiring, a double beat which may only be that of the clock. But the demon of analogy seizes him again, sensations are superimposed, and an overlay of absurdly beating wings is sketched on the beat of the expiring pendulum. Could it be some nocturnal bird, some frightened guest of the night? No, it is rather a rustling, "le frottement familier et continu d'un âge supérieur" (the familiar and continuous rubbing of a superior age). His entire line of ancestors appears before him, the whole throng of apparitions that he had reincarnated during his nights of insomnia. Their crowded presence constitutes the shadows of his past.

Doubt is no longer possible. "La certitude se mire en l'évidence" (certitude is mirrored in the evidence). Even as the only real beating is the pulsation of his own heart, the only

4 The same contrast between light and shadow can be found in a sonnet dated July 2, 1868: "De l'orient passé des Temps" (From the long-past Orient), the first version of the famous sonnet of 1885, "Quelle soie aux baumes de Temps" (What silk embalmed by Time). Born from the analogy hair/drapery, and containing most of "Igitur's" images (Time, Nothingness, curtains, darkness, waves), the sonnet ends thus: ". . . ces beaux cheveux / Lumineux en l'esprit font naître / D'atroces étincelles d'Etre, / Mon horreur et mes désaveux." (. . . this beautiful hair / Luminous, gives birth in the mind / To atrocious sparks of Being / My horror and my disavowals.) (Cf. *Fontaine*, No. 56, and *Les Lettres*, special issue, pp. 182–83. The two reviews obviously inverted lines 7 and 8 in their successive printings of the text.)

clarity which endures is *self-awareness*, infinitely reflected in
that abstract place where the past and the future come face to
face like two reflecting panels. It is, in truth, the "reflecting
chamber" of initiatory tradition. In a decisive division, this
awareness, or consciousness, is separated from its Shadow. This
Shadow is composed of every shade of his race, each one in turn
suppressed and laid to rest under the darkness of oblivion; and
it is also the last figure, which now appears as an enigmatic,
vague personage in the light of consciousness. Its velvet-covered
bust is topped with a ruff; its face remains invisible, since it has
"no consciousness of itself" and is the *"subconscious of its
race."* The mysterious message of this race has been locked
under an heraldic clasp in the volume in his hand, "the volume
of his nights."

So, without leaving the room, but by descending the stair-
case of the human spirit, Igitur has gone, as the Argument
notes, "to the very bottom of things." From spiral to spiral, he
has explored his subconscious, all the while remaining at the
summit of himself in the Absolute.[5] Yet, in this eternal instant
when he seems to have attained supreme indifference, he
clearly feels that he must *do* something to identify fully with
the Absolute: make a gesture, perform an absurd, mad act.
Since every human act is subject to chance, *he rolls the dice*,
and chance is negated by that very act, for one number, and
not another, is projected on the firmament; one Idea, and not
another, is manifest in accordance with its own necessity. In
short, the Infinite, the great unlimited and indeterminate All,
is finally fixed in this simple movement. Where? Naturally, in
the "grimoire," the sorcerer's book, the volume that Igitur had
to hold open in order to accomplish the Act when he "forgot
human parlance" and consigned the Dream inherited from his
ancestors to its pure state.

Having justified man by imitating with a roll of the dice, the

5 The apparent contradiction between the title and the contents of
Chapter II of "Igitur" can be resolved by referring to the version of Chapter IV published after the scholia by Dr. Bonniot: "Having arrived at the
Absolute as an adolescent, he had not experienced the steady climb of the
concept; its inverted march was a spiral, alternately illuminated and in
darkness, at the top of which he lived as an Absolute, incapable of moving."

mysterious and primordial gesture which created the constellations, Igitur can, so to speak, reenter the Absolute. He closes
the book and drinks of the phial in which his dream has finally
died, and which now contains only "the substance of Nothingness." Crossing his arms, he "blows out the candle" of consciousness, thus proving that man's supreme dignity is to be
able, of his own accord, to renounce his difference.

This would seem to be as near as one can come to the meaning of this very important work. So far its hermeticism does
not seem to have brought out the best in many commentators.
There are certainly still many obscurities in the interpretation
proposed here. If a better knowledge of Mallarmé is desired, a
rigorous exegesis of this work should be undertaken, particularly
in the light of Hegel's philosophy (or at least as much as
Mallarmé knew of it) and the so-called esoteric traditions.
For the poet was undoubtedly inspired throughout "Igitur" by
both, in the symbolism of the room and the stairs as well as
in his dialectic between Infinity and nothingness and his concept of the sorcerer's book.

More important here, however, is the clarification that "Igitur" affords of what this last notion represented for Mallarmé.
At the beginning and at the end of the tale, we encounter two
closely linked images: the sorcerer's book and the moon. The
moon is the image of the Absolute which exists "beyond and
above time" (Introduction), and this luminary, the receptacle
of "thought" and of the Spirit, "lights up the dream he is in"
(éclaire le rêve où il en est). Its light is reflected in the "chimerical clarity" of the host's face, which, illumined by mystery,
seems to sum up the essence of all things. Having carefully
kept the vacant book in his hand closed, so that "all similar
impressions" contained in the unconscious of his race would
"amass" in it, the host's function is now to open it in order
to project the world of essences into it by a unique Act. This
roll of the dice transforms the empty book into a sacred sorcerer's book with an heraldic clasp, such as he had dreamed of six
or seven years earlier: a sorcerer's book containing all human
mystery and "science," which would "reproduce the logical
constitution of the universe," as Lefébure had once written to
Mallarmé, and fix Infinity.

A work, a Book so conceived, allowed no room for chance. Baudelaire had formally stated, "There is in the Word something *sacred* which prohibits us from making it into a game of chance." Even in 1866, Mallarmé was insisting to François Coppée, who had just sent him his most recent collection of poems:

Chance does not bring on a line of verse. Several of us have arrived at that, and I believe that, however perfectly the limits are drawn, what we must especially aim at is that the words in the poem, which are already sufficiently themselves not to receive any further impression from the outside, should reflect upon one another until they seem no longer to have their own color but to be only transitions in a scale.

Much later, Mallarmé would speak of words "lit up by their mutual reflections." Words would be so many mirrors, and the poem a reflection chamber reproducing the world in miniature. Mallarmé's theory of the poem was enriched from year to year, as we shall see. His life for the next thirty years was a long and continued meditation on this theme. From this moment on, liberated from his obsessions by "Igitur," he felt a "new man" being born in him. He knew that his intuitions of 1862 had not deceived him: The Book, the sorcerer's book, the Great Work, whatever its name might be, would henceforth be his sole task.

6 · Mallarmé, Cosmic Poet

Oui, je sais qu'au lointain de cette nuit, la Terre
Jette d'un grand éclat l'insolite mystère . . .
        "QUAND L'OMBRE MENAÇA . . ."

(Yes, I know that in the distance of this night,
    the Earth
Casts the rare mystery of a great light . . .)

I. SETTLING IN PARIS. "TOAST FUNÈBRE"

It was 1871. While the atmosphere in northern France was growing calm again after the war's tragic defeats, Mallarmé convalesced from "a supreme winter of anxieties and struggles." He, too, had his "terrible years." Looking back, he evaluated his evolution since his 1866 discoveries: "Those critical hours allowed me to see in flashes what my often-compromised four-year-old dream consisted of. I have it now, almost." He was aware then of the wealth of that dream, which had created a kind of "sea grotto" within him, and he would not lose it: "From it I am saving material for four volumes, opinionated and miserly, which will be my life" (to Mendès, May 22, 1870).

But he knew also that he should not undertake his work prematurely: "Begin right away, no. First I must acquire the necessary talent and make what I produce mature, immutable, instinctive, almost of yesteryear and not of yesterday." For the moment he would only help the Work to create itself "by means of appropriate labors." With this in mind, he had been studying linguistics for two years. His correspondence with Lefébure reveals his concern with the origins of language and the symbolic value of sacred languages, a study which shortly led him to conceive of and refine new poetic techniques. At the same time he contemplated undertaking a thesis at the Sorbonne, "dedicated to the memory of Baudelaire and Poe." For he also had to consider bettering his family's material situation, especially since a second child was about to arrive.

But a doctoral thesis is a long-term job; and besides, how could he escape mediocrity as long as he stayed in the heart of the provinces? With the return of self-confidence during those months of convalescence, Mallarmé felt ready for any and all adventures. He had already obtained a six-month leave for reasons of health and hoped that work with a publisher or in a library could be found for him. It scarcely mattered what the job would be, provided that it delivered him from the nightmare of classes and papers to grade. His friends were setting themselves to the task and would doubtless succeed. Meanwhile they offered lavish counsels of prudence: "If you have nothing—nothing but the hope of earning 3000 francs by working—take care!" wrote Mendès. "By and large, living by the pen is death. Oh! come if you can, but come to live, not to die!"

But Mallarmé ignored this and chose to regard his desires as realities. In May, 1871, he arrived, as he had so long yearned to do, in Paris, bringing with him his family, his furniture, and desk drawers full of vague outlines.

Stéphane Mallarmé has arrived—kinder, more polite, and madder than ever, with absolutely unintelligible prose and verse, a wife and two children, of which one is not yet born, and *without a cent.*

So Leconte de Lisle announced in a letter to Heredia the silent arrival in Paris of the man who fifteen years later would create such an upheaval in the world of letters. For the moment Mallarmé was looking for an apartment for his family and a way to support them. Fortunately, he found both in less than six months. At the beginning of November, the new teacher at the Lycée Fontanes and his family, the latter now increased by a baby boy, moved into a small apartment on the rue de Moscou.

Mallarmé's move to Paris did not, in fact, take place unnoticed. This poet of inoffensive mien had already begun to intrigue people. The second *Parnasse contemporain*, which had been held up by the war, published the "Scène d'Hérodiade." Even connoisseurs were astonished by its mysterious radiance. *L'Art libre* in Brussels printed strange prose poems which had escaped notice until then: "Plainte d'Automne," "Frisson

d'Hiver," "Pauvre enfant pâle," "La Pipe," and "Réminiscence."
His translations of Poe, appearing in *Renaissance artistique et
littéraire*, seemed no less strange, especially "The Raven," with
its typically Mallarméan sonorities:

*Une fois, par un minuit lugubre, tandis que je m'appesantissais,
faible et fatigué, sur maint curieux et bizarre volume de savoir
oublié—tandis que je dodelinais la tête, somnolent presque: soudain
se fit un heurt, comme de quelqu'un frappant doucement, frappant
à la porte de ma chambre—cela seul et rien de plus.*

He was seen sometimes at Leconte de Lisle's, sometimes at
Mendès', sometimes at Nina de Villard's or at the dinners of
the "Vilains Bonhommes" (Naughty Goodfellows), where he
met the literary eccentrics: Verlaine, Rimbaud, Charles Cros.
His conversation was already both charming and disconcerting:

Mallarmé has become madder than ever. . . . The moon bothers
him. He explains the symbolism of the stars, whose disorder in the
firmament seems to him the image of chance. But the moon, which
he contemptuously calls "that cheese," seems to him to be useless.
He is seriously dreaming of a wiser age of humanity when the moon
can easily be dissolved by chemical means. The only point that
troubles him is the cessation of tides, for the rhythmic upheaval of
the sea is necessary to his theory about the symbolism of the human
décor. Alas, poor human reason! (F. Coppée's unpublished journal,
quoted by Henri Mondor, *Vie de Mallarmé*, p. 328.)

On the contrary, poor Coppée! He had no idea that Mallarmé
was hiding serious research behind this apparent leg-pulling.
For reasons that are difficult to determine, the moon, whose
sobs had rocked more than one of his youthful poems, such
as "Apparition" and "les Fleurs," was from that time on
banished from his poetry; but the rest of the world at least had
begun to take on order for him. After six years of poetic silence
and physical and emotional convalescence, his horizon enlarged,
and the entire universe erupted in his work. "Toast funèbre"
(Funeral Toast), an occasional poem written at the request of
Catulle Mendès in Brittany during the summer of 1873, for a
"tombeau" in memory of Théophile Gautier, exemplifies this
evolution. It also magnificently marks his return to poetry.[1]

1 Commentary: Noulet, pp. 210, 378; II, p. 3. Mauron, p. 118; II, p.
172. Soula, p. 169. Gengoux, p. 77. Davies, p. 13.

"Toast funèbre" uses more than ever before his technique of superimpression. The visible theme is Gautier's death. But behind this, in filigree, is drawn Mallarmé's face and, on a larger scale, the face of every poet, of the Poet, of whom Gautier is the symbol, as in the first line:

> O de notre bonheur, toi, le fatal emblème!

> (Oh, you, the fatal emblem of our happiness!)

The first part of the poem consists of echoes of "Igitur" and even of the 1866 sonnets. In this entombment of his friend, Mallarmé relives his own experience: the death-throes of the self, among the chimeras, writhing in the half-shadow, up until the moment when one puts out the torch, blows out the candle of consciousness, and lies down on ancestral ashes. All this is still present when he has the idea of giving this "Funeral Toast" with its contradictory title and sketching a "salute of madness" to combine in a single homage the themes of glory and death. No, in lifting that goblet, in the depths of which some chimerical monster still suffers, he does not hope to resurrect the dead and bring back his shade, a magical apparition, through the room's corridor. The empty goblet, reminiscent of the "pur vase d'aucun breuvage" (vase innocent of any beverage), symbolizes Mallarmé's poetry and, as J. Gengoux says, pure Art or Form. Mallarmé is saying: We who have come together to sing the absence of a poet know very well that he is really and totally dead; he lives on only through his glory, which is merely the reflection of the Spirit, in the same way that the porphyry tomb where his body rests, bathed in the glow of sunset, reflects the sun's rays and sends them back to their source.[2]

2 To my mind, not a single commentator has offered a satisfactory interpretation for lines 12–15. Soula sees in the "feux du pur soleil mortel" (rays of the pure mortal sun) "the ardent inspiration of a still-living poet." For Mme Noulet, "the writer's glory returns through the evolution of art, to take its place in each day's light." G. Davies only sensed the analogy Mallarmé established between Gautier and the sun. Only Mauron saw that this was a real symbol, and that through that reflection of light Gautier seems to restore to the sun what it has given him. But he seems not to have seen that the sun here very precisely symbolizes the Spirit, and that only its rays symbolize glory. We shall have occasion to return to this symbolism.

Little by little the image of Gautier in his glory is superimposed upon and substituted for that of Mallarmé in his death-throes. In a second part, Mallarmé contrasts the dead Gautier to the throng of living humans and confronts him with nothingness. This throng, haggard before death and full of false pride in its own individuality, ordinarily says, "We are the sad prefiguration of the specters we shall be later." But Gautier, on the contrary, "magnifique, total, et solitaire" (magnificent, whole, and solitary), has been transformed by death into a hero, while the vain and impossible dialogue of nothingness and space reverberates in the night:

> Vaste gouffre apporté dans l'amas de la brume
> Par l'irascible vent des mots qu'il n'a pas dits,
> Le néant à cet Homme aboli de jadis:
> "Souvenirs d'horizons, qu'est-ce, ô toi, que la Terre?"
> Hurle ce songe; et, voix dont la clarté s'altère,
> L'espace a pour jouet le cri: "Je ne sais pas!"

> (Vast chasm brought in the fog's bulk
> By the irascible wind of the words he did not speak,
> Nothingness to this abolished Man of yesteryear:
> "Memories of horizons, what, oh thou, is the Earth?"
> Shouts this dream; and, a voice whose clarity is impaired,
> Space has for a toy the cry: "I do not know!")

But at the same time, the best of Gautier endures. Mallarmé endeavors to show the meaning of his work in a third part, a kind of sketch of an Art of Poetry in which Gautier seems to join with him in an ideal synthesis. He had proposed, with "Toast funèbre," "to sing the seer who, placed in the world, looked at it; which no one had done." Gautier, now the Master, had not only known how to look at and contemplate Nature with his "profound eye"; he had also understood it. His art conferred ideal meaning on Nature. Each anxious, trembling, Eden-thirsty flower that he encountered in "les jardins de cet astre" (the gardens of that star), he translated into a mysterious essence to which he was able to give a name: Rose, Lily. This is what lives after the poet: the glory of having performed his simple poet's duty, of having isolated the pure notion of each flower "dont nulle ne se fane" (of which none fade) from the multiplicity of appearances, in a vibration, a solemn agitation of words. The easy dream is excluded; this is the very definition of true poetry and the function of the "pure poet."

Despite the many penetrating comments that "Toast funèbre" has provoked, it still contains numerous obscurities. However, these difficulties do not prevent one from admiring it. To the reader they seem less like the effect of a gratuitous game than the expression of a great inner richness. It is a poem of radiant density, heavy with ten years' experience and meditation. In it Mallarmé put to the test a wholly new poetic technique, especially characterized by what Scherer so excellently calls "false imprecision." But Scherer suggests that this false imprecision is merely a "tendency to the blurred, the vague, the mysterious" which later bloomed fully with certain Symbolists. But we should also note a very conscious effort to confer on each element of the line that *polyvalence* already mentioned, which gives each sentence both depth and resonance. In the six lines quoted above, all the principal syntactical procedures that Mallarmé used ever increasingly are already to be found. First, he breaks with the habitual, lazy logic of prose by using brutal disjunctions: "Vast chasm" is in apposition to "nothingness," which comes two lines later; the verb "shout" is held over until the line which follows the sentence spoken by "nothingness," etc. Then he establishes unexpected ties between two images or notions apparently foreign to one another: the "irascible wind of words," "memories of horizons," the "cry" which is space's "toy." Finally, insofar as language permits it, he uses equivocal constructions: "shouts this dream." "This dream" could, at first glance, be either subject or object. Thus each word becomes a crossroads, a center from which multiple rays emanate. In short, Mallarmé was concerned from this point on with using language to produce those marvelous laceworks which would express the order of the world. He had been dreaming of them as long ago as 1866, when he compared himself to a sacred spider.

II. "LA DERNIÈRE MODE" AND THE FAUN'S AWAKENING

In 1875 Mallarmé was finally settled in life as well as in literature. It is unlikely that he felt that his moment had come. But there is no doubt that, after so many years of withdrawal and extreme cerebralism, the faun in him awakened, exuding life.

1875 was the year that he moved to the rue de Rome apartment, which his famous "Tuesdays" would soon make renowned. In that year he discovered a verdant corner, dear to painters, on the banks of the Seine, not far from Fontainebleau: Valvins, where he rented the first floor of a cottage on the river. Valvins and the rue de Rome became the two poles of Mallarmé's modest universe; solitude and social life. The poet soon revealed his exquisite qualities for the latter. Léopold Dauphin said later,

> No one has that precious gift of making himself loved more than he. He speaks and one is captivated; everything about him is attractive: his deep gaze, the gaze of a child's eye but full of dreaminess; his voice, warm, musical, melodious, sometimes fluty, like Banville's; his gentleness, his urbanity, his politeness; all his manners are simple and perfectly distinguished and his eclecticism judicious and good.

Beyond a few intimates, not many at that time suspected that this courteous and gentle exterior concealed a literary revolutionary. The publication of "le Démon de l'Analogie" in the first issue of the short-lived *Revue du Monde Nouveau*, launched by Charles Cros in 1874, enlightened a few others. It created havoc in literary milieux. Even the painter Manet, himself a revolutionary, grew worried. Mallarmé would later say of him in *Renaissance artistique et littéraire*, in the syntax that he was developing: "Monsieur Manet, for an Academy (and I mean by that what unfortunately, in this country, every official parley becomes) is, from the point of view of execution no less than of the conception of his paintings, a danger."

The warm mutual friendship of Mallarmé and Manet—both misunderstood, both revolutionaries in spite of themselves— consoled them for the public's lack of understanding. Jacques Scherer has pointed out that the two have a similar way of juxtaposing all the elements of a work to bring about a vital interplay from which the pure concept emerges. Speaking of the "only man who has tried to open new doors for himself and for painting," Mallarmé was at the same time thinking of what he himself had wanted to do for poetry, and also, in a most unexpected form, for prose.

It was during the summer of 1874 at Valvins that Mallarmé corrected the proofs of *La Dernière Mode* (The Latest Fashion). Its first issue appeared in September. This magazine seems at first a strange undertaking for a poet. Actually, it is less astonishing when one considers how much feminine preciosity there was in Mallarmé's character, and how he had been dreaming of founding a review ever since his arrival in Paris. As far back as 1872 he had undertaken to gather funds to underwrite a luxurious publication, *l'Art Décoratif*. The project never materialized. This time he planned to succeed. From fortnight to fortnight, he published eight consecutive issues and performed a tour de force by writing it completely alone, with the exception of tales or poems requested of friends. Under the pseudonyms Miss Satin, Marasquin, Marguerite de Ponty, Mouthpiece of Brabant's, his articles encompassed everything: cooking, fashions, theater, travel, and correspondence with his feminine readers which abounded in advice about dress, the choice of trinkets, and the education of young girls.

One wonders at this. But the lonely man of the nights at Tournon took pleasure, several years later, in meticulously annotating the changes of fashion and planning out excursions and recipes because he had a need for playfulness. After years of withdrawal and meditation, a natural law of compensation was finally liberating the other Mallarmé, the poet full of preciosity and grace who had written "Le Petite Laveuse blonde" and "Placet futile." More than one article reveals this in the turn of a phrase.

Even an inattentive reading of this magazine shows its intention to pursue Parisian existence in its pleasures and obligations, everywhere, ceremonious or intimate.

Thus does mere Paris amuse itself at summing up the universe, a museum as well as bazaar. There is nothing she will not accept, however strange, nothing that she does not sell, however exquisite. . . .

An almost unique column today: for, devoted at first to festivities, it finally treats only of solemnities and pleasures that are truly rare. . . .

La Dernière Mode was, then, connected with the poet's deep-est preoccupations. For him there was now nothing that was not of interest; everything could take on the air of a festivity, if not a "solemnity" (later that became the title of a "divaga-tion" [digression]). Even the most apparently frivolous object was charged with meaning for him. Nor is it astonishing that he who had once wanted to write a *Treatise on Precious Stones* should devote an encomium to jewelry in the very first "fashion chronicle":

Let us seek the isolated jewel, the jewel in itself. Where? Every-where. That is, a *little bit* on the globe's surface and *very much* in Paris; for Paris furnishes the world with jewels. What! Doesn't every region, like a flora by its very nature, present us with a complete jewelbox from the hands of man? Is the instinct for beauty and for relationships between diverse climates, which regulates the produc-tion of roses, tulips, and carnations under every sky, foreign to the production of earrings, rings, and bracelets? Flowers and jewels: has not each species something like its own soil? A certain flash of sunshine is suitable for this flower, a certain woman for this jewel. This natural harmony ruled in the past but seems abolished at present.

What was to be done was to go back through the medium of thought to the time when the "natural harmonies" were still known. In fashion as elsewhere—as in poetry—the essence of things must be resurrected. A necklace?

A thousand diamond letters sparkling with the captivating bril-liance of a *secret that is shown but not surrendered:* stringing to-gether the first and last names of the woman wearing the necklace and the man who gave it to her. Legend has it that a jeweler makes these necklaces and varies the formula of their mystery.

Is this not the very principle of Mallarmé's poetry transposed? The surprising article on the "mobile ceiling of a rented apart-ment" is even more revealing. Mallarmé proposes an arrange-ment of beams and boxes, "a rich, exquisite, bizarre ceiling" to mask the "sky customarily offered to the guest's eye," which is how he sees the usual ceiling, "whiter and more vast than a sheet of paper without a poem." His proposal would conceal the wretchedness typical of apartments and would contribute to forming the "Site." This was perhaps, too, a means of conjuring away his old obsessions by transforming Igitur's room into the ideal site that would be evoked in "Prose pour des Esseintes."

An effort to create a new language can also be discerned in these bits of bravura. Words are disposed in an unpredictable order so as to light up one another with their separate flashes, as in the sentence which concludes one article with a kind of burst of fireworks:

Brillante imagination, n'est-ce pas? qui rappelle les métamorphoses mêlant à des gazes d'insectes un visage de femme dans les albums anciens de Grandville: non, elle appartient au génie de ce magicien extraordinaire, lui aussi, mais autrement qu'en des vignettes, ordonnateur de la fête sublime et quotidienne de Paris, de Vienne, de Londres et de Pétersbourg, le grand Worth.

(A brilliant idea, is it not? which recalls the metamorphoses mingling with insect gauzes the face of a woman, in the old Grandville albums: no, it belongs to the genius of that magician who, he too, is extraordinary, but elsewhere than within the frame of a vignette—that director of the sublime and daily festival of Paris, Vienna, London, and St. Petersburg, the great Worth.)

Scherer notes quite exactly that "under this charming disguise, Mallarmé can risk anything. . . . Thanks to the touch of preciosity that this genre requires, he can venture innovations that do not appear peculiar. . . . *La Dernière Mode* . . . is the first truly Mallarméan work." Let us say that it is at least the first work in which a Mallarmé appears who is relaxed and liberated from his anxieties and funereal obsessions.

This explains why, despite his first failure, Mallarmé thought of resurrecting the "Faun," which had been lying dormant in his desk for ten years. After the *Troisième Parnasse contemporain* refused it, he chose to publish it privately. He said of it later: "One of those first costly pamphlets; a candy bag, but made of dreams . . . somewhat oriental with its Japanese felt, title in gold, and tie knots of black and Chinese pink." It was not yet the Book, the Great Work, but it was a book, *the first he had published*, and because of this we can imagine that nothing was left to chance. "Mallarmé put together his book's appearance with the same attention and taste that he gave a dress in his *Dernière Mode*," comments Mme Noulet perceptively. "L'Après-Midi d'un Faune" was probably in his mind an opportunity to give material reality to his theories on books as well as to his new principles of language.[3]

In fact, a careful comparison between the "Monologue" and "l'Après-Midi" discloses even better than "Toast funèbre" the characteristic procedures that Mallarmé employed thereafter to create what Scherer calls the "depth of the sentence" and give his poems a sort of third dimension through the interplay of superimpressions and polyvalences. First of all, he substituted for words of pure description terms that were equivocal but also harmonious. For example, the forest's "foliage" becomes the Faun's "doubt":

> O feuillage, si tu protèges ces mortelles,
> Rends-les moi, par Avril qui gonfle tes rameaux
> Nubiles . . .
>
>   (Monologue)

(O foliage, if you protect these mortals,
Give them back to me, by April who swells your nubile
  branches . . .)

> Mon doute, amas de nuit ancienne, s'achève
> En maint rameau subtil . . .
>
>   (l'Après-Midi)

(My doubt, heaped up from a distant night, is consummated
In many a subtle bough . . .)

The precise plural ("tes rameaux," your boughs) is generalized in the "maint" (many a) which Mallarmé used more and more to suggest rather than describe. "Nubiles" is replaced by "subtil," which strangely lightens the line without changing its vowel sounds.

The typography creates the impression of superimposed levels and relief with its italics, its capital letters (CONTEZ, SOUVENIRS), and especially its blank spaces, suggesting background planes of thought and dream:

> Réfléchissons ...
>   ou si les femmes dont tu gloses
> Figurent un souhait de tes sens fabuleux!

(Let us reflect ...
                  Or what if those women you criticize
Embody only a wish of your fabulous senses!)

3 Commentary: Thibaudet, p. 393. Noulet, p. 228.

Typography, punctuation, choice of words, suppression of verbs: everything conspires to give "l'Après-Midi" an impression of lightness and evaporation that is missing in the "Monologue." So does the syntax, with its inversions, pauses, and parentheses, which make the verse flit like the nymphs pursued by the Faun:

> Si clair,
> *Leur incarnat léger, qu'il voltige dans l'air*
> *Assoupi de sommeils touffus.*

> (So bright,
> Their incarnate lightness, that it flits through the air
> Drowsy with tufted sleep.)

But it is not only the form that has changed; the theme has been altered too, although the pretext and the conclusions remain the same. Mme Noulet has shown in her minute comparison of the two texts that the first faun tries again to get hold of and materialize his desires, while the faun of 1875 endeavors to reshape his memories in order to give them a more spiritualized explanation. "J'avais des nymphes! . . . Où sont-elles? . . . Je les veux!" (I had nymphs! . . . Where are they? . . . I want them!) said the first faun. And the second: "Ces nymphes, je les veux perpétuer" (Those nymphs, I want to perpetuate them). All the difference is there. A profound transformation of the poet separates one from the other. It was now Mallarmé's intention to show that the only true reality is spiritual: that of the ideal world in which individuals are lost and only the pure essence of things endures: "la faute idéale de roses" (the ideal lack of roses).

As we already know, it is the poet who allows us access to this ideal world. The faun, who ten years ago was merely a young adolescent full of sensual desire, now incarnates the poet whose inspiration quickens all things. The murmuring water one seemed to hear is, in fact, the sound of his flute; and the only apprehensible wind,

> *C'est, à l'horizon pas remué d'une ride,*
> *Le visible et serein souffle artificiel*
> *De l'inspiration, qui regagne le ciel.*

> (It is, at the horizon undisturbed by a ripple,
> The visible and serene artificial breath
> Of inspiration regaining the sky.)

Thus "l'Après-Midi" becomes an Art of Poetry without the
name, according to which the flute, the reed-pipe, the pipes of
Pan as symbols of poetry, "instruments of flight," somehow lend
consistency to dreams and create the translucent world through
which the poet considers appearances:

> Rieur, j'élève au ciel d'été la grappe vide
> Et, soufflant dans ses peaux lumineuses, avide
> D'ivresse, jusqu'au soir je regarde au travers.

> (Laughing, I lift to the summer sky the empty grape-cluster
> And, blowing into its luminous skins, avid
> For intoxication, until evening I look through it.)

The universe, thanks to its transmutation in this poetic vision,
bursts into an exalted celebration of spirit just as it is about to
disappear.

> À l'heure où ce bois d'or et de cendres se teinte
> Une fête s'exalte en la feuillée éteinte.

> (At the hour when this wood is tinted with gold and ashes
> A celebration flares up in the burnt-out foliage.)

The funereal silence of midnight, when Igitur's burial took
place, gives way to the "proud silence of noon," to which the
poet-faun now succumbs in the slumber of satisfied desire.

III. IN THE SHADOW OF THE "TOMBEAUX"

The publication of "l'Après-Midi d'un Faune" would seem
to mark Mallarmé's definitive entrance on the literary scene.
In that same year, he became the Paris correspondent for the
English review, The Athenaeum, and published Beckford's
Vathek, an eighteenth-century oriental tale, written in French
by an English lord. Mallarmé added his own obscure and provocative preface. He also made several translations of Poe for
the République des Lettres, headed by Catulle Mendès, which
he himself had helped to organize. In any case, Mallarmé's activity was completely devoted to England at that time. A trip
to London the previous summer had provided the opportunity
for renewing his friendships with various English poets, among
whom were O'Shaughnessy, Bonaparte, Wyse, and Swinburne.
The last invited his collaboration on a new "tombeau" being

prepared across the Atlantic in honor of Poe. Mallarmé on this occasion would have the opportunity of expressing in immortal verse his devotion to the man who was still his great master of poetry: "Tel qu'en Lui-même enfin l'éternité le change" (When into himself eternity changes him).[4]

The brilliance and astonishing density of "Toast funèbre" is here concentrated in the fourteen lines of a sonnet. Several of them are true crystals and the entire poem a "calm block" glimmering with infinite facets. Here too, abstract and concrete are constantly mingled, and each image, each word, gives rise to a whole system of poetic ideas.

The key to the sonnet lies in the first tercet: to sculpt in the imagination an "ideal" bas-relief for Poe's tomb ("our idea"). The mutual hostility of ground and cloud,[5] earth and heaven, is symbolized by the struggle between the hydra and the angel, i.e., the throng of his contemporaries and the unknown, misunderstood Poet. From this arises an effect of superimpression which recalls the three sonnets on Beauty. Here again, the *absence* of a bas-relief is designed to suggest more effectively, not the corporeal image of the poet, but the "idea" of Poe. Poe symbolizes the Poet, angel of the Spirit in general, at grips with "le bétail ahuri des humains" (the bewildered herd of humans), which becomes the "siècle épouvanté" (the terrified century), the hydra with a hundred heads. In this ideal portrayal, the Poet is seen (as he was in the youthful piece, "Contre un Poète parisien") armed with poetry as if with a naked sword. (The original version said, a naked "hymn.") He provokes his century by endeavoring to awaken it, "le susciter," to itself, by virtue of an unknown language, in a strange voice which would restore "les mots de la tribu" (the words of the tribe) to their pure, original meaning. Death's triumph, changing everything into eternity, is thus affirmed, whereas the crowd had chosen to see this poetry as mere sorcery, the product of alcohol rather than of genius. But again, this is only an ideal bas-relief. In reality, "the tomb of Edgar Poe" consists of a simple block of

---

4 Commentary: Thibaudet, p. 228. Noulet, pp. 247, 390. Mauron, p. 168. Gengoux, p. 87. Davies, p. 89. Chassé, *Rev. litt. comp.*, Jan., 1949.

5 My interpretation is similar to that of G. Davies, and in contradiction with those of other commentators.

black granite, calm as an immobile landmark. The last tercet situates it in a grandiose, cosmic perspective. It seems not to have been made by the hands of men, but to have "chu d'un désastre obscur" (fallen from some obscure disaster). This gigantic meteor, erect on the empty earth, is destined to protect the poet's memory from future blasphemies, already eddying, scattered, in the sky.

The theme of death summoned Mallarmé again a few months later and awakened forgotten resonances in his subconscious. It would seem, as Charles Mauron has indicated in his *Psychanalyse de Mallarmé*, that the sonnet "Sur les bois oubliés" (On forgotten woods) was written in memory of Ettie, the girl who had inspired "Apparition" when she was engaged to Cazalis and had later married Lefébure's friend, the historian Maspero. The poem [6] contains the décor of the nights of Tournon and, beyond that, of childhood reveries such as "Ce que disaient les trois cigognes": winter, forgotten woods, solitude, the ultimate funeral flames, the sepulcher. However, an impression of calm serenity prevails. The young woman's shade is speaking. It explains the conditions for her appearance to the man who weeps for her: no "heavy bouquets" on the grave, because their mere material presence would prevent him from summoning the dead woman. He may not listen to the tolling of midnight, fateful hour of death and absence, and he must be content with calling her name. In accordance with the theory expressed in "Toast funèbre," the pure idea of the absent loved one will arise through the miracle of poetic incantation.

> Pour revivre il suffit qu'à tes lèvres j'emprunte
> Le souffle de mon nom murmuré tout un soir.

> (To relive, it suffices that I borrow from your lips
> The breath of my name murmured for a whole evening.)

These exquisitely harmonious lines express once more the soul of the poet, the "anima" which had dictated "Apparition" and "Soupir" fifteen years earlier.

Finally, one other sonnet seems to be contemporary with the

6 Commentary: Noulet, p. 391. Mauron, p. 168; II, p. 17. Davies, p. 89.

preceding one in its composition and images: "Quand l'ombre menaça" (When the shade threatened).[7] It is not, properly speaking, a "tombeau," but, like the others, it revolves around the themes of death and darkness. First, it retraces and condenses Mallarmé's experience very accurately in four magnificent lines: the struggle with the old dream of a personal afterlife, "désir et mal de mes vertèbres" (desire and pain of my vertebrae), which finally folded its wing. But the setting is no longer the room. As in "Toast funèbre," it is scaled to the universe, the "salle d'ébène" (ebony room). There the constellations, those famous garlands, are dying and yet still attempting to attract man, the king of creation. It is a vain endeavor, because the poet illuminated by truth, the "solitaire ébloui de sa foi" (the lonely one dazzled by his faith), knows full well that the external world is nothing but lies and empty pride. There is only night and, in its depths, an unprecedented mysterious light: Earth, resplendent not through its own material brilliance but through human genius, poetic genius. This luminous pinpoint in the boredom of limitless and unvarying space endows all of creation with its value and meaning.

These three pieces and "Toast funèbre" constitute, almost indisputably, the summit of Mallarmé's total work. No other poem sums up his vision of the world with more dazzling density. No other lines better embody his ideal of a poetry in which words "light up by mutual reflection," each one, in its place, finding its primitive purity again. At thirty-five, Mallarmé appeared to be in full possession of his art and his genius. The last poems he had written should assure him of uncontested glory. What kept him from publishing a collection of his poems?

Instead he was silent for another six or seven years. The "Tombeau d'Edgar Poe" was published only in Baltimore, among other homages in English. It did not appear in France until 1883, with the sonnet "Quand l'ombre menaça," and then thanks to efforts on the part of Verlaine. "Sur les bois oubliés" remained unpublished until after the poet's death. Why? Because not one of them yet constituted the Work he dreamed

7 Commentary: Noulet, pp. 251, 404; II, p. 44. Mauron, p. 153; II, p. 170. Gengoux, p. 58.

of. He considered them not even fragments, but merely occasional poems, "studies with better in view," as he later said. He remained faithful to the solemn contract he had made with himself ten years earlier: "I will need twenty years." His correspondence attests to his intrepid perseverance: "My labor advances. Shall I attain the goal I have set, alive and not dead of starvation? Darkness . . ." And four years later to Gustave Kahn: ". . . Paris, where I have been living more aloof than ever, hunched up over a great work of several years" (to O'Shaughnessy, July 4, 1877).

What, then, preoccupied him? The Work, of course, and more precisely the theater. In 1876 he was "in the process of putting together the scenario of a very big popular melodrama" which never saw the light. The following year he claimed to be working furiously on a new kind of theater. His interest in *Hamlet* led him to dream of a drama with a single character.

It was a false start, however, and the years that followed saw him cloistered again. At long intervals, the English teacher of the Lycée Fontanes whose works were viewed by his Principal as "strange lucubrations" and "foolish productions" simply published more scholarly books. In 1878 there appeared the *Petite Philologie à l'usage des Classes et du Monde: les Mots anglais* (Brief Philology for the Classroom and the Public: English Words), and, in 1880, *Les Dieux antiques, "nouvelle mythologie illustrée"* (Ancient Gods, a New Illustrated Mythology). These works, which he would later call "professional jobs, nothing more . . . nothing to be talked about," were perhaps not so foreign to his poetic preoccupations as it might appear.

It has been demonstrated that the *Mots anglais* reveals extensive research into the nature of language and especially the expressive value of sounds and letters. For example, comparing language to a living organism, he says, "The Word presents something like flesh in its vowels and its diphthongs; and in its consonants, a skeleton delicate to dissect." There is a trace of esoteric doctrine in this declaration. Similarly, he notes that in English the letter "f" "forms with 'l' the majority of words having to do with the act of flying or flapping," while "d" "expresses a continuous, nonexplosive, deep activity like digging, diving, or dropping, as well as stagnation, emotional heaviness, and darkness." Such reflections certainly influenced his poetic creation. In the following lines of a sonnet composed at this time, he was perhaps seeking to transpose his remarks on English to French:

> . . . *la pierre que mon doigt*
> *Soulève avec l'ennui d'une force défunte?*
>
> (. . . the stone that my finger
> Lifts up with the lassitude of defunct strength?)

It is even plausible that his research in the English language had some influence on his poetic vocabulary and his very syntax. Charles Chassé (*Lueurs sur Mallarmé*, p. 101) has noted in this regard Mallarmé's frequent use of "maint" and "aucun," which resemble the English "many" and "any," as well as the anglicism of usually placing the adjective before the noun.

Dieux antiques would also seem to reveal the preoccupations of a poet in quest of an explanation of the world. As George Cox, whose thought Mallarmé interpreted while translating him, put it:

. . . I would say that Mythology is simply a collection of the "they says" by which men of olden times told one another everything they saw or heard in the countries where they lived. This explanation, or key, which has opened almost all of Mythology's secrets for us, has been put into our hands by science only in the last few years. We moderns can notice, then, better than classical peoples, to what extent these "they says" in their primitive form were natural and at the same time endowed with marvelous beauty and truth (*Oeuvres complètes*, p. 1164).[8]

Mallarmé can even be caught bridging his various studies. For example:

Languages and myths are never so completely transformed that the two sciences of Language and Mythology cannot rediscover, by their recent efforts, the original kinship of words and gods (*Oeuvres complètes*, p. 1170).

What is the Poet's task, if not to discover this original kinship, and, in his research on the myths of the past, to "learn many a symbol"?

---

8 Translated from Mallarmé's own, rather free version of the English.

Even in these "professional jobs," Mallarmé is never too far away from the road he had chosen. Besides, for one who has once perceived the unity of the world, everything is good.

It was thus that Mallarmé was "more aloof than ever, hunched up." The literary world around him was spinning with activity. The rebels proclaiming their hatred of the bourgeoisie were no longer isolated and few, as in the time of Nina de Villard. Groups of agitators were forming in the cafés of the Latin Quarter. The "Hydropaths" and later the "Hirsutes" brought the avant garde of poets together, while Laurant Tailhade, Rollinat, Jean Moréas, and Verlaine, who had just returned to literary life, launched their offensive in the pages of the review *la Nouvelle Rive gauche* (New Left Bank). Mallarmé remained distant from the excitement. His Tuesday evening salon did welcome several young poets attracted by his conversation and those lines of his poetry with which they were familiar. Some, like Gustave Kahn, sensed in him the Master from whom one word would suffice to impose his authority and doctrine on that noisy, inconsistent world. But Mallarmé, withdrawn and in mourning over the cruel deaths of his cherished Manet and Nina de Villard,[9] pursued his task in silence. He did not suspect that the time was at hand when the glory that he sought so little would unexpectedly descend upon him.

9 Manet died in April, 1883, and Nina de Villard in July, 1884.

III. The Master of Symbolism

7 · The Discovery of the Symbol

> "Mallarmé spoke, like some supremely initiated priest, of the symbol."
>
> RENÉ GHIL

I. THE PERIOD OF "THE DECADENCE."
"PROSE POUR DES ESSEINTES"

Mallarmé might have anticipated that glory. In October, 1882, he had received a letter from J.-K. Huysmans, who wished documentation on the poet for the preparation of his next novel, in which the hero was to be the last descendant of a great race. The following summer, Verlaine, renewing their old friendship, announced that he was about to publish a series of studies on the "Poètes maudits" (Accursed Poets), in whose ranks he planned to number Mallarmé. The studies were to appear in *Lutèce*, formerly the *Nouvelle Rive gauche*. He requested "something unpublished, quickly, quickly!" Shortly after, Mallarmé answered Charles Morice, who was also pressing him:

I would need to talk for ten minutes to explain to you that I have no new unpublished verse, in spite of one of the most enormous literary labors yet attempted, because I am so deprived of leisure that I am devoting my time to the framework of my work, which is in prose. We have been such latecomers in thought that I have spent no less than ten years in constructing my own (November, 1883).

This important declaration divulges why he had written no poetry for more than five years, and why his activity for the coming years would be essentially devoted to prose. His research into language and mythology, his meditations and conversations also showed the necessity of reinforcing the edifice of his thought to give his work a solid structure. So he postponed

creating it until later, when he would finally have the leisure to
devote himself to it totally. It mattered little to him that the
immediate present offered him the opportunity to be exposed
to a wider public and finally to acquire celebrity with a few
new poems. He would make no concessions to easy glory at this
point, any more than he would have done ten or twenty years
earlier. He had projected a certain route for himself and would
simply follow it.

For Verlaine's article he barely consented to search out of his
desk drawer a few old poems such as "Placet" and "le Guignon,"
together with the unpublished "Apparition," "Sainte," "Don du
Poème," and "Cette nuit" (This Night; later "Quand l'ombre
menaça"), to which he added the "Tombeau d'Edgar Poe." At
that, he felt the need to rework them to a sometimes unrecog-
nizable point so that they would conform to his present principles.

The publication of "Les Poètes maudits," first in *Lutèce* and
then in a small volume, was quite an event for the literary
world. For the first time it became evident that a major transformation in French poetry had been in preparation for some
years. The much-scorned Mallarmé was not alone: Cormière,
Rimbaud, and Verlaine had tried to rise up against ready-made
thought and poetic conformity. But the author of "Hérodiade"
and "l'Après-Midi" already stood out as their leader. Verlaine
honestly and humbly effaced himself before the man in whom
he recognized a master and "the gigantic effort of this poet so
badly received by the critics." In spite of the critics, Mallarmé's
work represented to him one of the summits of French poetry.

Mallarmé expressed his thanks as soon as the book appeared:
"I have nothing behind me that is worth anything other than
through the superb enhancement of your sympathy, my dear
Verlaine, nothing, or almost nothing, truthfully. . . ." This
modest statement is misleading, for fame had already come. In
a few months, it would become almost glory, thanks to Huysmans' novel *A Rebours*, which, in its author's own words, fell
"like a meteor into the literary marketplace." The hero,
Floressas des Esseintes, owed a great deal to Mallarmé. The
poet had once told Huysmans stories about the extravagant
activities of his friend, Robert de Montesquiou, that modern

Fantasio forever in quest of more refined sensations. In return, des Esseintes, an eccentric inhabiting a fairytale setting where he composes gustatory symphonies with his "mouth-organ," delights particularly in reading Mallarmé's poems: "This condensed literature, this quintessential juice, this sublimation in art" strikes him as a marvelous incarnation of "the decadence of a literature, irreparably stricken in its organism and in haste to express everything in its decline."

At the outset, then, Mallarmé was classed with the "Decadent" poets. The term was already dear to the Romantics, and Verlaine had used it unwittingly in a sonnet which evoked the "Empire at the end of the decadence." The short-lived "Decadents" grew out of this use, and thanks to them the adjective gained notoriety. In 1884 it was on the lips of all those in Verlaine's entourage in the cafés of the Left Bank. He was already acknowledged as the leader of the new "school." As for Mallarmé, it is probable that he was not displeased by his association with the emulators of des Esseintes. Several months after the publication of A *Rebours*, in January, 1885, he presented the *Revue Indépendante* with a provocatively obscure poem entitled, equally obscurely, "Prose pour des Esseintes" (Prose for des Esseintes).

None of his poems has excited so many diverse and often contradictory interpretations.[1] This is because he practiced hermeticism quite deliberately from that moment on. Can he be accused of a wish to mystify? He clearly took pleasure in sending his reader off in the wrong direction; but this is only one of the aspects of his art, one intention among many others. In fact, the obscurity would seem to stem from his efforts to confer a third dimension on his work through multiple, superimposed meanings. He increasingly employed a vocabulary that he had created, a repertory of images which, in his mind, had taken on an eminent value, corresponding to the many and complex networks to which he alone possessed the key. What appears unintelligible to the uninstructed reader must have often seemed clear, or at least comprehensible with some effort of concentra-

1 Commentary: Thibaudet, p. 403. Noulet, pp. 254, 412; II, p. 58. Mauron, p. 122; II, p. 177. Soula, p. 29. Gengoux, p. 25. Chassé, *Quo Vadis*, November, 1949.

tion, to him. He said of Theodor de Wyzewa, one of his young disciples and commentators, "He is charming, but why does he explain my verse? That tends to create the impression that it is obscure."

If it is not to be "obscure," the reader must identify with Mallarmé's universe, and to do this requires a complete exegesis of his work. "Prose pour des Esseintes" admittedly remains very obscure to this day, despite the numerous commentaries that have sprung up around it. All that can be attempted is to extract the general dialectic and avoid searching for a single, unilateral interpretation. Most critics have been guilty of this attempt, which merely impoverishes the poem's meaning.

The title, visibly meant to perplex the reader, is the first victim of this error. What sort of "prose" is this, written in octosyllables? Some say: prose, simple narration. Others suggest a sort of liturgical hymn. But why choose? Mallarmé evidently conceived of this piece in a narrative vein, as an exception to his custom, but this in no way excludes the possibility that he did want to confer on it a liturgical aspect which conforms perfectly to his concept of poetry.

Moreover, the first two stanzas have a solemn and almost religious tone. They constitute a real program of optative poetics. The narration which follows is an example of how to use this poetics. Hyperbole: the secret, the touchstone of poetry: "A leap beyond, a jump toward something else" (Mauron); "metamorphosis of the natural into the supernatural" (Noulet); or even, as Mallarmé himself said, "transmutation of the fact into the ideal." May this hyperbole rise, spring up from the poet's memory and the memory of the race's past, and triumphantly assure the realization of the "grimoire," [2] the Book! As Camille Soula has shown, Mallarmé is the man possessing "the science of mystery" which transforms landscapes into "sites," as in an atlas. Real flowers become ideal flowers as in an herb museum, and everyday words are changed into the magical language of

2 E. Noulet confers on this word the meaning of "confused language," which seems to me impossible in the light of the discussion in Chapter 5. Certainly it is not clear why the sorcerer's book is bound "with iron," when previously Mallarmé had referred to the golden clasps on old missals. But does this justify an interpretation which obviously runs counter to *every other* use Mallarmé made of the word "grimoire"?

rituals. After this profession of faith, which magnificently clarifies the poet's mission to inaugurate "the hymn of spiritual
hearts," Mallarmé gives an example of such a transmutation, in
an apparently anecdotal manner.

Two people are taking a walk on an island of abundant
flower gardens. Who is the mysterious companion whom the
poet designates in turn as sister and child? A woman, probably
Méry Laurent, according to Thibaudet and Mauron? Or a
personified abstraction (consciousness, according to Soula; the
unconscious, according to Gengoux; patience, according to E.
Noulet)? Here again, why choose, when the very theme of the
piece is hyperbole? As in "Toast funébre" and as always,
Mallarmé undoubtedly uses a precise memory as a springboard.
In this case, it was a real walk with someone dear to him, who
may very well have been Méry Laurent, whom he liked to see
as both mistress and sister. The walk must have begun with a
courtly, gallant conversation in which the poet compared his
companion's charms to the beauty of the landscape. But the
comparison had a magical effect. Suddenly the landscape was
transformed before his eyes. Its "charm" had worked at the
same moment that his companion took on a new face. Stanzas
four and five express this, in a general evocation of the effects
of this hyperbolic transmutation, but in such a condensed, en-
tangled form that any attempt at discursive explanation becomes impossible. What seems most plausible is that such a
change goes beyond human reason for the poet. "L'ère
d'autorité se trouble" (The era of authority is disturbed). This
very real southern landscape, with its well determined number
of flowers (one hundred irises), has swiftly become a nameless
site, but one which is designated by "L'or de la trompette
d'Été" (Summer's golden trumpet), i.e., the voice of triumphant poetry.[3]

The following stanzas detail the vision. "*Oui,*" on that island
where "*pourtant*" (yet) any hallucination of the senses is im-

3 It seems to me indisputable that "site" is used here, as elsewhere, in
the sense of the ideal place, Eden, the garden of Ideas. And why could it
not be the antecedent of "que cite" (which . . . cites) rather than, as
it at first appears, the word "nom" (name)? This conforms to one of
Mallarmé's habits and gives what seems to me the only plausible interpretation of this stanza.

possible, the poet and his companion, mute with astonishment,
watch the flowers grow disproportionately, to the point where
each one seems to live "in itself," independently and separated
from the soil, adorned with a "lucid contour," exactly like those
of "Toast funèbre," which were isolated by the poet's gaze
"between the hour and the light of day." The key stanza, the
peak of the poem, follows: the flowers appear as what they are,
Ideas of flowers, the glorious accomplishment of the poet's long
and patient craving:

> Gloire du long désir, Idées
> Tout en moi s'exaltait de voir
> La famille des iridées
> Surgir à ce nouveau devoir . . .

> (Glory of my long desire, Ideas
> Everything in me exulted to see
> The family of irises
> Arise to this new duty . . .)

When the appearances of the world seem to vanish before
our insistent gaze, this ideal duty, as "Toast funèbre" put it,
consists of distinguishing beyond them the Essence of things,
their pure idea.

While the poet exults, his companion, a sane and tender
sister, is content to smile enigmatically, as if in ecstasy. He
tries to understand, to "hear" her smile. He desires then that
the Spirit of contention, the will to discern, in him as in us,
may know in this supreme hour (not of Midnight but of Noon,
the time of the poetic transmutation of all things) that the
multiplicity of appearances vanishes to give way to a vision
of unprecedented dimensions, outside of all reason. Meanwhile,
common man stays "on the bank," where he monotonously
laments his daily life and refuses to understand how the poet
can be so astonished. In his companion's smile, the poet had
"heard," perceived, that the map, the atlas, the sky, the entire
ideal world which he had awakened underfoot (like Gautier in
"Toast funèbre"), confirmed by his vision, represented a land
that never materially existed![4] All that remains for the sister-

4 My interpretation of these stanzas is quite distinct from any other.
Not enough attention has been paid to the "sister's" successive attitudes.
In particular, the verb "ouïr" (to hear, line 45) should be tied in with

child to teach him is the "word" of all poetry: Anastasis! In Mallarmé's memory the word radiated the splendor of oriental decadence, but he clearly chose it to heighten the notion of hyperbole stated at the outset. "Arise!" she says to the poet, seeming, not without humor, to be calling him by name. "From this absence of everything, bring forth the ideal world through poetic transmutation, and fix it in the eternal parchment of the sorcerer's book." After that she has only to die, and her sepulcher will reveal her true identity: Pulcheria, i.e., Beauty, carried within the poet and discovered by the attainment of pure consciousness. This Beauty is hidden in the vision of the disproportionately enlarged ideal flower: "le trop grand glaïeul" (the too-great gladiolus).

Several months before the publication of "Prose pour des Esseintes," Mallarmé had replied to a request for a definition of poetry:

> Poetry is the expression of the mysterious meaning of the aspects of existence through human language brought back to its essential rhythm: in this way it endows our sojourn with authenticity and constitutes the only spiritual task.

Was this not, in advance, the best possible commentary on the poem that was about to appear?

II. A SYMBOLIC POETRY

The *Poètes maudits*, *A rebours*, "Prose pour des Esseintes": Mallarmé had become famous in less than a year. He was insulted or jeered at by many, but others revered him as a new god. In spite of himself, he had given the battle cry. Several months later, the poetic revolution broke out.

There were already those who every Tuesday deserted the Left Bank cafés, where Verlaine held forth among the most restless of the young poets, for the little salon on the rue de Rome. Here friends and admirers came in increasing numbers

---

the verb "entendre" (to hear and understand, line 35). Then stanza 12 becomes a revelation typical of Mallarmé, on the condition—which in him would not be surprising—that "ouïr" has both a direct object, "tout le ciel et la carte" (the whole sky and the map) and an object clause, "Que ce pays n'exista pas" (That this land did not exist). The sky and the map are only an anticipation of "this land."

to hear the gospel. Moréas had given the signal, with Louis le Cardonnel. Then came the group of Wagnerites, with Dujardin and Wyzewa and Fénéon, both of whom worked on the *Revue Indépendante*. René Ghil followed at the head of a band of very young men recently graduated from the Lycée Condorcet, who had been overwhelmed by the "revelation" of this new poetry. Finally came Maurice Barrès, young director of *Les Tâches d'Encre* (Inkspots), who was the first to give, in a few lines, a more or less valid explanation of Mallarmé's art:

He simply aspires to gather a whole poem in one line... Let us follow his method of composition: Taking a singularly complicated initial idea, he refines upon it mathematically. Then, to realize it, having made the choice of some rare and *adequate* comparison, he suddenly lets everything go and keeps only the comparison, from which he launches, without further explanation, into new and more distant analogies. Also, to tighten the whole thing, he suppresses transitions; and most often he proceeds, not from idea to idea, but from emotion to emotion... Proudly conceived lines sown here and there acquire a superb brilliance from the very obscurity of their foundation. This symbolic poetry is a stimulant which does not quench. . . . (*Les Taches d'Encre*, December 5, 1884).

Symbolic poetry: the word Mallarmé had been seeking so long had suddenly appeared fortuitously in the writing of an admirer. It was soon to be brandished like a flag. Barrès may indeed have borrowed it from Mallarmé himself, whom René Ghil portrayed then as speaking, "like some supremely initiated priest, of the symbol."

Mallarmé gave two new samples of this "symbolic poetry," an interpretation of the aspects of the universe and essential rhythm, to the *Revue Indépendante* in March, 1885. The first, "Le vierge, le vivace et le bel aujourd'hui" (The virginal, vivacious, and beautiful today), one of his most beautiful and famous poems, is probably, as Mme Noulet thinks, a new version of an older poem. Without the manuscript it is impossible to determine how much it was reworked.[5] However, in this embodiment of a theme which no longer corresponded to his present attitudes, he undoubtedly introduced at least certain

5 Commentary: Thibaudet, pp. 217, 249. Noulet, p. 263; II, p. 86. Mauron, p. 157; II, p. 166. Gengoux, p. 61. Wais, p. 570.

procedures which generalized the value of the central image: syntactical condensation: "La région où vivre" (the region in which [ ] to live); abstraction: "qu'à ce lieu son pur éclat assigne" (which its pure brilliance assigns to this place); or a gripping synthesis of images: "Le transparent glacier des vols qui n'ont pas fui!") (The transparent glacier of flights that never flew!)

Be that as it may, the poem is more difficult to understand than a first glance might indicate. Too many commentators, relying on a rapid reading, have made Mallarmé's swan the romantic symbol of the poet imprisoned by life and men. This slights the subtle dialectic in the sparkling interplay of images and the value of the three tenses used: past, present, and future. The "swan of once upon a time" ("un cygne d'autrefois") is the Mallarmé of the Dream, of Igitur's wintry boredom—not the lucid winter prior to "Hérodiade," but the sterile winter after the crisis of Tournon. If that crisis had not again instilled in him the impotency that Igitur had to exorcise, the poet would have been able to take his flight, enriched by his new experience and his vision of Beauty, to "sing of the region to live in," i.e., the ideal site to which his pure brilliance destined him. The swan at present has lost none of his brilliance, but his failure to take flight at the right moment has imprisoned him in his own dream, long since rigid around him like a transparent and frozen lake. At this point, the poem opens, like a sudden rip, and is projected in leaps and bounds toward the future:

> Le vierge, le vivace et le bel aujourd'hui
> Va-t-il nous déchirer . . .

> (Is the virginal, vivacious and beautiful today
> Going to tear for us . . .)

The swan is there, still magnificent, but covered with frost like the lake. Drunk with space, he beats his wing. Will he be able to break the ice and free himself from a sterile dream to find his real homeland, that of the authentic poet who creates his own ideal site? Alas, the struggle is hopeless. His neck will succeed in shaking off the frost, his spirit, denying space, will fight against the agony that it inflicts; but the wing of inspiration will remain the prisoner of the ground. Thus the poet, a scorned phantom of himself, is immobilized forever in the horror of the sterile dream in which he has fixed himself.

This symphony in "I" major is the triumph of an entirely conscious art which unites suggestion of an idea with precision of form. Nevertheless, it seems to admit of a defeat to which Mallarmé would probably no longer subscribe today. In fact, the other piece he published in March, 1884, "Quelle soie aux baumes de temps," had quite another sound. This is an entirely new version of the 1868 sonnet, "De l'orient passé des Temps," discussed earlier in the present study. In it Mallarmé repeats the analogy hair/draperies, but, significantly, in combination with the analogy hair/flag of the earliest text, "le Château de l'Espérance." In so doing he seems to conjure away the impression of horror that had haunted him seventeen years earlier by reintroducing the sensual, ardent, exalted Mallarmé of twenty. Here the Chimera, symbol of the old dream, dies away in the folds of the flags or of some ancient cloth as if in folds of the past ("embalmed by time"). Meanwhile, the bare and defenseless mass of hair of the beloved is offered to the poet. The two tercets indicate a violent return to eroticism, despite the deliberate ambiguity of the form. The bite of the kiss, the cry smothered in the hair, everything evokes the triumph of physical voluptuousness through Mallarmé's two symbols of "glory" and "diamond," whose meaning is henceforth transformed into an evocation of the supreme ecstasy of love.[6]

This was the work of the "demon of noon" which had thrown Mallarmé a year before into the arms of Méry Laurent. He had met her at the home of Manet, whose mistress she had been. A minor actress turned model, she was then Mallarmé's neighbor on the rue de Rome. At thirty-five, she was at the height of her beauty: blond, elegant, lovely, surrounded by the quiet luxury of charming appointments. Everything about her was calculated to charm the poet, who rediscovered his youthful enthusiasm and early inspiration by her side. After long solitude, Mallarmé had finally come upon a happy period. Relaxed and abandoning himself to the desires of his body, he

6 Commentary: Noulet, p. 427. Mauron, p. 194; II, p. 208. Soula, p. 151. Gengoux, p. 185. Wais, p. 595. B. Fleurot in *Les Lettres*, special issue, p. 185.

also listened once more to his soul. Amidst the increasingly worked-over hermeticism of his poems, he allowed an occasional glimmer of graceful preciosity.

And so, at the very same time that he was composing "Prose pour des Esseintes" in 1884, he published the poem on Mademoiselle Mallarmé's fan in the *Revue Critique*. Here again he indulged in metaphorical superimpression, but this time with all the ease of a great lord. Like "Prose pour des Esseintes," but less ambitiously, the poem constitutes an Art of Poetry:

> *O rêveuse, pour que je plonge*
> *Au pur délice sans chemin . . .*[7]
>
> (Oh dreamer, so that I may plunge
> Into pure pathless delight . . .)

"Autre Éventail" (Another Fan) brings about the synthesis of the four themes most purely typical of Mallarmé: the fan itself, the wing, the dream, and the line of poetry. The fan speaks, and its *apparent motion* is visibly the starting point of the poem. It comes and goes, making the air tremble and creating coolness all around it. It seems to spring out unceasingly, but it is really a prisoner of the hand that manipulates it and closes it up into its folds. This motion reminds the poet analogically (as it already had, in "Placet futile") of the opening and closing of the wing of a bird which, despite its efforts, cannot escape. Thus, two series of images interweave in counterpoint. At the same time, the hand holding the fan belongs to a young girl, the "dreamer" who really controls its back-and-forth motion. Her soul, a laughing but timid paradise, slides into the folds and hides: a subtle lie since she seems to let the wing go, only to pull it forever back again. The movement is then only the appearance of motion, a kind of great kiss, "fou de naître pour personne" (wild at having been born for no one), a pure, gratuitous effervescence without a destined end.

The poem's interpretation could be limited to that worldly, subtle game, were it not for the first word: "dreamer." The reader is incited from the beginning to identify the girl dis-

7 Commentary: Noulet, p. 410. Mauron, p. 131. Gengoux, p. 166.

creetly with the poet, thus confirming the image of the wing as the symbol of poetic inspiration. From then on, the fan becomes the poem, and the beating of the wing becomes the verse, always ready to escape, but always held back by the poet's exacting genius. The lie is subtle because it seems to make the horizon recede and create a new universe, a space trembling with love. Actually, the poem closes in on itself. Its white and shuttered flight keeps its secret in its unanimous fold: an ideal site, a mysterious rosy paradise, reposing on golden evenings of inspiration as a folded fan rests against the sparkle of a bracelet.

In this poem, Mallarmé attains the most refined, the perfect achievement of his art. In a rustle of syllables in which sibilant and fricative s's, f's and v's interreact with e's and i's in elusive relationships, the poet manages, through the most frivolous, delicate object, to suggest the paradoxical nature of every poetic act: the promise always followed by a refusal, the suggestion of a universe which, if it disclosed its secret, would lose its mystery and hence its very existence.

III. THE REVELATION OF WAGNER

The publication of Mallarmé's provocative new poems in the first months of 1885 was, in spite of the reactions they aroused, partially obscured by the attention then being paid to a new god, Richard Wagner. His death two years earlier had attracted a flood of foreign admirers to Bayreuth and Munich, among whom were Édouard Dujardin and several of his young poet friends. Upon returning to France, he founded the *Revue Wagnérienne* and considered asking Mallarmé to be its spiritual director. At the last moment he may have feared creating a sensation. In any case, its contents were almost exclusively provided by those who already liked to be known as the "mardistes" (Tuesdayists). In this way, Mallarmé's direct influence began to make itself felt. It was to benefit at the same time from the Wagnerian vogue.

Yet Mallarmé was practically totally ignorant of Wagner. Dujardin, in the company of Huysmans, introduced him to this music one Good Friday at the Concerts Lamoureux, which he promptly began assiduously frequenting, with the result that six months later he wrote a long study in prose for the review, entitled "Richard Wagner, a French Poet's Reverie."

The article is both a critical study and a declaration of faith. Mallarmé admitted that he was fairly unfamiliar with Wagner and spoke of him as a poet who had long been meditating on the theater. Wagner's greatest merit for him was to have elevated the theatrical performance to the dignity of a cult, exactly as Mallarmé himself had envisioned it. He was referring to a truly magical cult, since its point was to convey the illusion of reality to the spectator through the sorcery of art. Wagner's great "find" was to have summoned Music to the task and married it to Drama. The "vitalizing sap" in Wagner's music first created "an atmosphere richer in Reverie than any air on this earth." Thus modern drama, like that of ancient Greece, was able to take the public's imagination back to the time of the legends and myths, inviting it to consider the secret of man's origins and bathe once again in the "primitive stream."

His admiration was shaded by certain reserves, however. Wagner's tumultuous music seemed to him to betray its object because it failed its own principle, of being "a vibratory background prolongation of everything." It certainly suggested a return to origins but did not allow a return all the way to the source, which is silence. In short, the Temple of Wagnerian art rose "halfway up the holy mountain," and its grassy lawn invited the pilgrim of the Ideal to come and rest. In contrast to this Germanic conception of art, the poet proposed a more French ideal, "strictly imaginative and abstract, therefore poetic." It would not evoke legends and anecdotes, but a unique Myth, a Type previously unnamed, a personage who would sum up in one gesture "our dreams of sites or paradise." At heart, while admiring Wagner, Mallarmé could not forgive him for having subordinated poetry to music. Although the authentic dramatist must obtain the "assistance of all the arts, to stir up the otherwise inert and nonexistent miracle of the stage," Mallarmé felt that only poetry was capable of performing this miracle. As he wrote to René Ghil, the duty of poetry was to "take everything back from music."

This long article was not enough for Dujardin. He asked the

Master for some poems and received them after a long wait. In the January 8, 1886, issue of the *Revue Wagnérienne,* the first of seven sonnets by French poets honoring the musician of Bayreuth was Mallarmé's "Hommage à Wagner."

The new poem does little more than repeat the essential ideas of the article. But Mallarmé had applied himself more than usual to interweaving many networks of images. Thus, some lines are almost incomprehensible, and it seems practically impossible to coordinate the various interpretations of the commentators.[8] Is Mallarmé contrasting the theater of the ancients to Wagner's (Thibaudet, Mauron)? Is he describing the passage from vulgar writing to hermetic writing (Gengoux)? Is he comparing the failure of his own attempt to the triumph of Wagner's art (Soula, Noulet)? Nothing permits an absolute decision. Or rather, an analysis of the various images leads to the search for an interpretation that will be richer and more complex, although still hazardous.

Gardner Davies has noticed that this sonnet, designed to commemorate the anniversary of Wagner's death, is another "tombeau." A temple of Wagnerian art is evoked by the words "pilier," "grimoire," "parvis," "vélin" (pillar, sorcerer's book, parvis, vellum), and finally "the god Richard Wagner, radiating a consecration." In this temple, mourning is late in coming, as in the beginning of "Toast funèbre": a fold of black drapery fallen on the furnishings gives substance to the funereal, forgetful silence, the "manque de mémoire" (lack of remembrance). The décor recalls from afar that of "Hérodiade," i.e., of the nights of Tournon and "Igitur." It also evokes the dying of the poet's dreams in the funereal draperies of that room. A parallelism is thus established between Mallarmé and Wagner, between the room and the temple, its furnishings destined to be forgotten and destroyed with the "settling" of the main pillar, i.e., with the disappearance of the Master himself.

Yet the Work cannot perish. For there is an object in the shadow, its presence barely suggested, whereas in "l'Ouverture" and "Igitur" it was clearly indicated, as it will be in the remainder of this sonnet: the "grimoire," the sorcerer's book,

8 Commentary: Thibaudet, p. 307. Noulet, p. 428. Mauron, p. 177. Soula, p. 49. Gengoux, p. 94. Davies, p. 131.

"aux pages de vélin" (with vellum pages), as "l'Ouverture" had said. There is "more than a single fold," then, on the furnishings: there is the sorcerer's book of many folds, or pages. Mallarmé treats this idea in the article, "Le Livre, instrument spirituel" (The Book, a Spiritual Instrument). There he emphasizes that the folding of a book has a quasi-religious value: it makes the book form a minuscule tomb for the soul, a silent depository of a secret made up of evocative, mysterious signs.

But here Mallarmé asserts that this "grimoire," this sacred depository, is the witness of our effort, Wagner's and mine, of our triumphant frolics. This Book is similar to the one dreamed of by the poet in "l'Art pour tous" (Art for All), with its inviolate hieroglyphics which seem to take flight by the thousands, thrilled to be causing, with the wing of inspiration, the shiver of art (that same shiver that was caused by the wing of Mlle Mallarmé's fan). The Book must not be destroyed. "Enfouissez-le-moi plutôt dans une armoire" (Rather than that, bury it for me in a cupboard), says the poet. The beauty of this somewhat unexpected line has, truth to tell, been disputed, but it seems to me that the poem hinges upon it. Far from expressing an avowal of failure, it proclaims, by contrasting "plutôt" (rather) with the idea of "précipiter" (to fling) into oblivion, the necessity of preserving the work from any injury, as a sacred depository. This line also introduces the concept contained in the tercets: it has been proved that the "grimoire" secretly contains Beauty; that from this silent, secret Book, the illusion of a world can at any moment spring forth in a grandiose simulation, just as in fact Wagner's genius sprang out of his score (that mysterious ink incapable of holding back his sybilline sobs, those vellums enhanced by gold) as if from primal chaos, amidst a symphony of creative clarion trumpets. And his immense figure dominates the open parvis of his temple, farther than the eye can see, "halfway up the holy mountain," while he is consecrated a god in the splendor of his glory.

The public's violent reactions to this sonnet are understandable, despite the beauty of these tercets, which suggest all of Wagner's orchestral wealth while fulfilling Mallarmé's dearest wish of twenty years' standing. Immediately upon appearing, the poem caused considerable reverberations. At Leconte de

Lisle's, everyone proposed an interpretation in turn, while only
the master of Parnassus refused to try to understand. At a
dinner of newspapermen, some made raucous fun of it while
others recited it in chorus. Without premeditation, Mallarmé
had just introduced an atmosphere of revolution into the world
of letters.

IV. THE SYMBOLIST REVOLUTION

Yet Mallarmé derived no pleasure from manifestoes or manifestations. When challenged, he allowed others to answer for
him. In *le Temps* of August 6, 1885, a certain Paul Bourde
attacked the Decadent poets in general and Mallarmé in particular with facile irony ("M. Mallarmé, who from his beginnings
was unintelligible, has remained faithful to himself"). Jean
Moréas lashed out with a noisy reply in which he brandished
the decisive word "symbol," which had already been mysteriously
pronounced for months on the rue de Rome. "The so-called
Decadents," he said, "seek above all else pure Concept and the
eternal Symbol in their art." Thus the critics should "more
correctly refer to [these poets] as 'symbolists.' "

After that, Mallarmé had no choice but to acknowledge his
effect and influence with his customary good grace. When
Verlaine requested several biographical details for his *Hommes
d'aujourd'hui* (Men of Today), Mallarmé sent him the following declaration of faith, later reedited under the title "Autobiography":

I have always dreamed of and tried for something else. . . .
What? . . . the Book, convinced that basically there is only one,
attempted unknowingly by whoever has written, even Geniuses.
The orphic explanation of the earth, which is the poet's sole duty
and the literary game par excellence: for the very rhythm of the
book, in that case impersonal and alive, even in its pagination, is
juxtaposed against the equations of this dream, or Ode.
This is the bared confession of my vice, dear friend, which I
have rejected a thousand times, my spirit annihilated or weary, but
it possesses me and perhaps I shall succeed: not in creating this
work in its totality—to do that one would have to be I can't imagine
who—but in showing one executed fragment, in making its glorious
authenticity scintillate in one spot, giving an indication of all the
rest, for which one lifetime is not enough. To prove by finished

portions that this book exists, and that I have recognized what I shall not have been able to accomplish.

And farther on:

At my long-vacant Tuesdays, your *Poètes maudits*, dear Verlaine, and Huysmans' *A Rebours* interested the young poets who love us (with the exception of the Mallarmists), and it was believed that I had attempted some influence where there were really only conjunctions. Very close in spirit, I was ten years ahead of the others in taking the direction in which similar young minds would turn today.

Shortly after, he visited Verlaine in the dismal hotel room which lodged him after he had left the hospital of Tenon. The two old companions-in-arms met with emotion. "Eh! Now we are famous, Mallarmé! Leaders of a school!" "Yes," replied Mallarmé, "who would have thought it!"

After twenty years' effort his hour had finally come. Appointed successively to the Lycée Janson of Sailly in October, 1884, and the Collège Rollin in October, 1885, he now bore more lightly the monotonous burden of teaching. The reports of official inspectors were less severe: "His calm and slow teaching has the merit of exactitude." More relaxed than twenty years ago, he enlivened his classes with anecdotes and occasional hilarious improvisations. Between the incense that rose before him every Tuesday from his growing troop of admirers and the passionate evenings in Méry Laurent's boudoir, he had found a balance—better, a reason for living.

"Victorieusement fui le suicide beau. . . ." (Victoriously fled the beautiful suicide).[9] . . . This sonnet, included in a letter to Verlaine and published in 1886 in *Hommes d'aujourd'hui*, indicates to what an extent he was now deliriously involved with strong sensations and triumphant images. After fifteen years of poetry devoted almost exclusively to "tombeaux," the fiery poet within awakened. References abound to gold, blood, glory, triumph, and tempest. But the precious poet reappeared too, he who had known at twenty how to play with his sensations and give them lightness and grace. The two are once more

9 Commentary: Thibaudet, p. 285. Mauron, p. 160; II, p. 204. Noulet, p. 432. Soula, p. 125. Gengoux, p. 227.

united, as they were when he was twenty, by the theme of the
mass of hair which gives birth through superimpression to the
theme of dusk. Mallarmé has seen the sun set in its glory.
It is midnight. Is he again to know the pains of dying and
death? No; this time, he is able to flee victoriously the idea of
moral suicide, and the last purple rays will drape an empty
tomb. For he is not alone on this night. Beside him a rich mass
of blond hair, "Trésor présomptueux de tête" (the head's pre-
sumptuous treasure) has replaced the flames of the setting sun.
This time he does not seek oblivion and nothingness in the hair,
which seems like a rain of roses, but "a little puerile triumph,"
—laziness, delirium, the sweetness of life, a trace of the vanished
sky and dream. Beyond the golden-helmeted mistress playing
at being a child empress, the sister of yore is evoked, the fairy
coifed in brightness from whose loosely clasped hands a bouquet
of stars snows down. For a moment, Mallarmé has found his
"anima" again, as at twenty, in the healing languor of love.

But did he not risk losing his poetry once more, and perhaps
forever, by complicating it even further? From this point on,
such long commentaries (and such lengthy discussions! for
despite all their ingenuity the critics have yet to propose a
satisfactory interpretation of the majority of pieces in the last
manner) would be required to explicate his poems that we
must settle for merely indicating several points of reference for
each one.

This is the case with a new sonnet,[10] published in Vogue in
June, 1886, which aroused laughter even in the depths of
Languedoc. The Mayor of Narbonne, perhaps facetiously, gave
several members of his administrations subscriptions to Vogue.
The first line of the sonnet, "M'introduire dans ton histoire"
(To introduce myself into your story) is intentionally equivocal
and lends itself to the most scabrous interpretations. The
poem's primary inspiration, like its predecessor's, is erotic. The
theme and principal images of the earlier poem are repeated.
But the play of superimpressions and syntactical entanglements,
plus the absence of any punctuation, give it an obscurity border-

10 Commentary: Mauron, p. 195. Noulet, p. 430. Soula, p. 157.
Chassé, R. H. L. F., July, 1952.

ing on hermeticism. And it must be admitted that the hermeticism is of dubious quality and constrains the critic to be content with conjectures.

The poet seems to be making excuses for his amorous liberties. He has made an assault on his companion's modesty, but it was as a frightened hero with the "talon nu" (naked heel) of ingenuousness, like the Faun of old. Yet that does not prevent him from bursting into joyous laughter at the sight of her hair and the way its glow pierces the evening air like a sunset. This time, a new image is superimposed on the double image of the hair and the setting sun: that of a royal chariot, specifically the Sun's chariot, but also, probably, the poet's, which, "tonnerre et rubis au moyeux" (with thunder and rubies in its axles), casts a vivid and triumphant light. It was the last blaze of love, perhaps the last blaze of inspiration as well, an inspiration which, thanks to rediscovered sensuality, was attempting to pass beyond the old obsession with virginity and impotency to express the ultimate transports of the world.

This joyous and triumphant inspiration appeared again in the sonnet "Dame, sans trop d'ardeur" (Lady, without too much ardor) and culminated in the poem "la Chevelure" (Hair), published the following year in *l'Art et la Mode*.[11]

Here the image of flight is superimposed upon the images that had occurred in the earlier poems: flames, desires, jewel, rubies, hero, glory, and an identical movement is expanded by the use of the alexandrine, in which each word seems to be mounting to the assault of love. The same analogy as before is simplified and reduced to its essence: the vision of the beloved woman apparently fuses with the vision of her hair, that darting flame flashing like a jubilant, protective torch in the shadow, "à l'extrême occident de désirs" (at the far-west of desires), which is continued and reflected like an inner fire in her gaze, and illuminates the poet's doubt with a new certitude.

While Mallarmé busied himself with these increasingly skillful exercises, the literary revolution broke out. In the *Figaro littéraire* of September 18, Moréas printed his famous mani-

---

11 Commentary: Thibaudet, p. 196. Mauron, p. 165. Noulet, p. 456. Soula, p. 141. Gengoux, p. 218. Chassé, *Figaro littéraire*, April 26, 1952.

festo, again insisting on the name "Symbolism" as "the only one that can reasonably designate the present tendency of the creative spirit in art." In reality, Mallarmé had himself given a rich, precise, and personal definition to symbolism a month before that of Moréas:

An disputable desire of my time is to separate, as if for different attributions, the two states of the word, the one raw and immediate, the other quintessential. . . .

What use is the miracle of transposing a fact of nature into a vibrating quasi-disappearance through the play of the word, unless the pure concept emanates from it, undisturbed by close or concrete associations?

I say: a flower! and beyond the oblivion to which my voice relegates any precise shape, inasmuch as I speak of something other than known blossoms, there arises musically the very, the suave idea of that flower that is missing from all bouquets (Preface to René Ghil's *Traité du Verbe* [Treatise on the Word]).

So, then, there are two languages. Besides the colloquial speech of "universal reporting," the poet creates a special, essential language. The question is no longer one of narrating, or teaching, or describing, but of *suggesting* the musical, suave idea, the pure notion beyond the peculiar reality, which it cancels, of every object. This is achieved by virtue of the line of poetry, which "uses several vocables to refashion a total word which is new, strange to the language, and so to speak incantatory." The very conditions of the Symbol were thus defined for the first time: poetic language, suggestion, music. René Ghil underlined the definition several pages later in speaking of "the real and suggestive Symbol" from which "the prime and last Idea, or Truth, will rise, whole and naked, palpitating for the dream." But best of all was Mallarmé's phrase, "l'absente de tous les bouquets." It summarized once and for all the theme of all his researches, from "les Fleurs" and "Surgi de la croupe et du bond" to "Prose pour des Esseintes."

8 · Above the Fray

> ". . . simply that I have renounced abstracting
> anything prematurely from my thought, from
> now until the day when I shall be permitted to
> produce in their strict and total clarity the several
> obsessive ideas which are still—yes, in spite of
> an entire lifetime!—confused or incomplete."
>
> CORRESPONDENCE

I. SOCRATES' LITTLE HOUSE

Five years sufficed to accomplish the Symbolist revolution.[1]
In 1886 the name itself had merely been a password among a
few of the initiated. By 1891, the press had accepted it, and
the new school's triumph was official. Mallarmé managed to
remain an astonishing paradox in this battle against literary
conformism and bourgeois common sense led by a handful of
poets in the name of an ideal of music and pure poetry. He
always refused to enter the lists or to print a manifesto, and
yet he was in fact the involuntary promoter and undisputed
victor in the battle.

Several years earlier, when he had formed the habit of gathering certain poet friends in his home each week, he certainly
had not aspired to become the leader of a school. But in the
long run, so great is the magnetic force of an original and long-
ripened mind, all the worthwhile young poets of the Left Bank
were gradually drawn to him. Henceforth, the small salon on
the rue de Rome could scarcely contain the Tuesday night
inundation. Latecomers to Parisian Symbolism, Henri de

---

[1] Revolution, not movement. As a movement, the French origins of
Symbolism go back to the first half of the nineteenth century, particularly
to Nerval and Baudelaire, who did much to prepare, and in part accomplished, the poetic revolution. But the historical revolutionary fact, the
collective awareness, is situated very exactly between 1886 and 1891. (See
my *Message poétique du Symbolisme*, Vol. II, and, on the distinction between literary movements and revolutions, my *Introduction à une Science
de la Littérature*, pp. 258 ff.)

Régnier, Francis Vielé-Griffin, Pierre Quillard, Saint-Pol-Roux, and André Fontainas, met there, as well as "independents" like Laurent Tailhade. Mallarmé's conversation also attracted guests from the provinces and foreign countries: the Belgians Albert Mockel and Émile Verhaeren; the Englishmen Arthur Symons and Oscar Wilde; and the German Stefan George. All eager for truth, they came several weeks or months in a row to hear what they felt was a new gospel.

Geneviève Mallarmé later recalled the simplicity of these gatherings:

The little diningroom was made ready immediately after dinner, for many arrived early, although most of them had to come all the way across Paris. The old Louis XVI table was folded up to a half-circle to make more room. On it were placed an old china pot full of tobacco into which everyone shortly dipped, cigarette paper, and a bouquet. Chairs were placed close together all around the table, for the room was quite small and the doorbell rang often. We adjusted the height of the overhead lamp, its brightness softened by a panel of Japanese crêpe. From a corner of the old sideboard, Lilith watched all these arrangements. The bell rang, Father opened the door himself, or if he were talking, I did. . . .

Lilith was the cat, the daughter of Banville's cat and the granddaughter of Gautier's. She was the last member of a whole dynasty of various animals which had succeeded Neige, the white cat from Tournon, in the poet's intimate surroundings: Frimas, Neige's son; Saladin, the long-eared Kirghiz greyhound, who had, his master said, the "bearing of an Asian prince," and who had once elicited from Manet the apostrophe, "No nonsense, now, that dog of yours will do me in for thirty thousand francs' worth of canvases." Then there were Iseult, the Italian greyhound, and Clair de Lune, the screech owl, not to speak of the "little academicians," Mallarmé's name for his enchanting green parrots.

Habitués and passing guests gathered around the table. Standing before the big porcelain stove under his portrait by Manet, Mallarmé let words and pipesmoke fall from his mouth. Jean Ajalbert described his voice, "rising, soaring in a sleepwalker's flight sustained by our breathing." There was little dialogue: in a contemplative silence, the "Master" improvised without a trace of pedantry. The improvisation leapt from subject to subject, a mosaic of fantasy and wit, light, profound, glistening, or flashing, but always impalpable.

What a luminous and flowering conversation is his, all crystal and roses! The whole younger generation listened to him as if to a precursor or one of the Magi. A savory voice. The gestures of an officiating priest. Words inexhaustibly subtle, ennobling every subject, and with rare ornamentation: literature, music, art, life, and even news items, uncovering secret analogies, doors of communication, hidden contours in things. The universe is simplified because he sums it up in the Dream, as the sea is summed up in the inner murmur of a seashell (Rodenbach, *L'Élite*, quoted by Mondor, *op. cit.*, p. 585).

Remy de Gourmont had this to say in his *Promenades littéraires*:

His words were received like those of an oracle. Really, he was a kind of God... A tribute from his mouth was as disturbing as a decree of Providence. I can still see Henri de Régnier flushing with emotion at one of the master's delicate compliments. It was a wonderful school of glory, one learned to set its rays above all other human distinctions. Perhaps only those who were disciples of Mallarmé can fully understand the profound meaning of the words in the life of a Greek philosopher, "He was a disciple of Socrates."

To be a new Socrates was exactly how Mallarmé saw his mission. Writing to Léo d'Orfer, he said, "It's been a long time since I have had the pleasure of seeing you on Tuesday: you know that you are always expected, since you are one of the oldest of the friends who so faithfully fill Socrates' little house" (June 30, 1888). He in no way claimed to teach a doctrine. He only wanted to teach others to meditate as he had done for twenty-five years. For this reason, no doubt, not one of his most fervent disciples managed to record anything more than snatches of his disconcerting, magnetic discourse. And yet a great lesson emerged for them all from every evening they spent together: the feeling of a supreme exigency and the conviction of the eminent dignity of poetry, raised to the heights of a religion. They perceived that the poet's mission was to decipher and express in verse the inherent mystery of the world.

So Mallarmé dreamed aloud every Tuesday, speaking of his

work in veiled words, as of a sacred task upon which he had
been meditating for twenty years without having yet been able
to undertake its realization. Gradually he created his own
legend and sustained it by refusing to publish a volume of what
he still considered exercises or occasional verse. The rare and
precious samples of this still unknown poetry that were scattered
in reviews were copied with veneration, exchanged with great
mystery, and prudently discussed in private. The most daring
hazarded a public presentation of their glosses, among them
the young Theodor de Wyzewa, who was supposedly one of the
spokesmen of the movement and the best interpreter of
the Master's thought. When Mallarmé published his famous
triptych of sonnets in the *Revue Indépendante,* Wyzewa thus
felt called upon to discuss them the following month in the
same review. The poet carefully refrained from expressing ap-
proval or disapproval. He remained above the fray, modest and
enigmatic. He enjoyed being surrounded by an aura of mystery
which was certainly not foreign to his growing glory. To each
request for his collaboration in a new review or manifesto he
sent a courteous refusal:

> . . . simply that I have renounced abstracting anything prema-
> turely from my thought, from now until the day when I shall be
> permitted to produce in their strict and total clarity the several
> obsessive ideas which are still—yes, in spite of an entire lifetime!—
> confused or incomplete.

II. A DRAMATIC CAMPAIGN

However, for a period of eight months (November, 1886–
July, 1887), he consented to deliver the first fruits of his meditations to the same *Revue Indépendante.* It is significant that
at this point he turned to prose. He had not given up poetry,
but he felt that he had to elucidate the "several obsessive ideas
which [were] still . . . confused or incomplete," before setting
about the definitive composition of the Work. By devoting
himself to criticism, he thought to bring a "noble complement"
to poetry. Hence came the first series of articles which would
become, with later writings, the collection *Divagations* (Digres-
sions).

The Critic's role is to meditate on poetry and art in general.

For Mallarmé, there was only one "single or pure art," only one art capable of "shouting its demonstration in practice": the theater. "The theater is of a superior essence," he said. Its function and eminent dignity are to represent "the play written in the folio of the sky and mimed by man with the gesture of his passions." Mallarmé's meditation here is unwittingly related to the Hindu concept of the theater as a Great Game, the best Game, a reduction of the order of cosmos, in which each individual is placed according to his rank and function. Through it the stage becomes "the majestic opening onto that mystery whose grandeur we are put into the world to envisage." He laments the absence of true theater from the stages of his day. "With an immense rent, the Goddess's veil has been destroyed." In this singular dramatic chronicle he preferred to expound, or at least suggest, in dense and often sibylline prose, his concept of the ideal stage Work, rather than to discuss the new plays of his time.

This ideal theatrical work should include dance, music, and poetry. Dance is, in fact, the concrete figuration on stage of every rhythm and every correlation implied in music. The dancer, a magician who seems to tangle, lead, or unwind a divining thread, is not a woman but a *metaphor*, "the visual incorporation of the idea." She represents a star. (Could she, he remarks, be better named?) The corps de ballet around her represents the ideal dance of the constellations. More specifically, mime strikes him as being closer to the principles than any other form of art. It does not present an effective action, but only an idea, "perpetual allusion without breaking the looking glass," a false appearance of the present. Somehow it achieves silence, the condition and delight of reading. The character of Pierrot, "a phantom as white as the not-yet-written page," is the very symbol of all poetic potentiality.

The ideal theater should not be made up of dance any more explicitly than of music. The great merit of Wagner was to have rehabilitated theater's sacred function and "cleansed it with the great musical water of the Temple." His error was to have sought to achieve a total art by mixing everything. For only poetry is total art. Theater, which is, after all, only poetry in action, should, like poetry, "take back what is good in

music." Music then, like dance, should be internal to poetry;
as Pierrot suggests, true poetic theater is, above all else, mime
and silence.

Mallarmé was gradually rediscovering, in more and richer detail, his preoccupations of the times of Tournon and Avignon,
the period when he was writing the scenario of "Hérodiade,"
the Faun's Monologue, and the "drama" of "Igitur." A name
on a poster brought out of his past the "adolescent who
vanishes from us at the beginnings of life": *Hamlet*. For
Mallarmé this name exercised a fascination bordering on
anguish. He was "that unique character in an intimate and
occult tragedy," the Hero par excellence, whose famous monologue had always been the play-type, the "Monologue or drama
with oneself." This Hero does nothing else but "walk around
reading in the Book of himself," in which he sees the ever-
alive testimony of "morbid duality." He discovers that he is
externally mad, but fixes "an image of himself within his eyes
that he keeps as intact as a never-drowned Ophelia." Hamlet, a
jewel preserved pure under his disaster, incarnates the "solitary
drama" of us all: that of "a latent lord who cannot become," a
stroller lost in a labyrinth of trouble and grief, a dream holding
an unachieved act forever in suspense. "For, know this well:
there is no other subject; the antagonism in man between dream
and the fatalities of his existence administered by misfortune."

The Work's meaning became more and more precise. It was
a *Solemnity*, a consecration, as Mallarmé liked to say: the
unique act consummated before and for an entire people,
which sums up the very drama of the world. In it the thousand
elements of Beauty that lie scattered, unknown, or detached
must be arranged in order according to their essential value; in
it the purest of ourselves, the metaphorical sky, "the spiritually
and magnificently illuminated heart of ecstasy" must be expressed.

It is understandable that the rare pieces that Mallarmé had
written or was writing seemed unimportant to him in comparison with this dreamed-of Work. However, upon the insistence
of friends and editors, he finally decided to produce a complete
edition of his poems, albeit a luxury edition of only forty-seven
copies, published by the *Revue Indépendante*. This time again,

the acquisition of Mallarmé's work would have remained the
privilege of a select few, had he not succumbed the same year
to the urgings of friends to contribute large excerpts, in the form
of a pamphlet, as part of the *Anthologie contemporaine des
Écrivains français et belges* (Contemporary Anthology of
French and Belgian Writers), published simultaneously in
Brussels and Paris. For the price of fifteen centimes one could
reread at leisure, if not "Hérodiade" and the "Faune," at least
"les Fenêtres," "les Fleurs," "Brise marine," "Soupir," "Sainte,"
the first prose poems, and four recent sonnets, all grouped under
the title *Album de vers et de prose* (Album of Verse and Prose).
Among the recent sonnets was "Mes bouquins refermés sur le
nom de Paphos" (My books closed on the name of Paphos),
just published in the *Revue Indépendante*, which would later
become the epilogue of his *Poésies complètes*.[2]

This poem, published in the review directly after the three of
the "Triptych," could seem also to have been composed twenty
years earlier, were it not for a totally different impression con-
veyed, one of serenity and ease. It too glorifies absence, but an
absence suggesting a new feeling: the savor of life. In reading,
the poet comes across a name full of evocative appeal: Paphos.
On this mere name used for his rhyme, Mallarmé seems to in-
tend to build his whole poem—his dream, a landscape of
ancient splendor, a ruin near the sea where goddesses are born.[3]
But then winter, the real landscape surrounding the poet,
comes "avec ses silences de faux" (with its scythe-silences),
with its snow frolicking on the ground to sweep away all these
visions. No matter. Why should he lament this effacement?
His spirit's hunger has no need of fruits, whether real or
imaginary. It needs only their savor, i.e., their very essence,

---

2 Commentary: Noulet, p. 444; II, p. 112. Mauron, p. 197; II, p. 181.
Gengoux, p. 160. Wais, p. 607.

3 Mme Noulet's commentary on line three is an excellent example of
Mallarmé's concision and density. About "Une ruine par mille écumes
bénie" (A ruin blessed by a thousand foams), she writes: "No detail is
superfluous. Each word, "mille," "écumes," "bénie," is historically or at
least legendarily legitimate. Astarte (bénie) was born in Paphos, emerging
from the foam (écumes) because the winds had especially agitated the
waters (mille) at that spot on the coast" (Stéphane Mallarmé, *Dix Poèmes*,
p. 116).

which will be born from their absence, "docte manque"
(learned lack). We understand, then, through the familiar
play of superimpressions and a return to the erotic vein, that
these fruits are nothing other than the two breasts of one of
the Amazons evoked at the outset by the mere name of Paphos.
One is bursting with flesh, symbolizing real life; the other,
burned according to the ancient rite to permit the drawing of
the bow, symbolizes absence. And it is on the latter that
Mallarmé, perhaps desperately, would prolong his dream.

As Mallarmé was finally deciding to publish, the new movement around him was seeking to formulate its doctrine more
completely by attempting to elucidate the metaphysical principles of its first pronouncements. Between 1888 and 1890, Paris
bubbled with mystical ideas, from the Left Bank cafés to the
Chaussée d'Antin, where the picturesque Edmond Bailly daily
welcomed the most convinced occultists in his *Librairie de
l'Art Indépendant*. Esoteric works swarmed into print: the
Traité Élémentaire de Science occulte (Elementary Treatise on
Occult Science) by Papus, who also launched the review *Initiation*; the preface to *les Grands Initiés* (The Great Initiates), in
which Édouard Schuré made a résumé of the "secret doctrine";
Georges Vahor's *l'Art Symboliste* (Symbolist Art), in which
the new school was defined as desiring to point out the miraculous analogies between the human microcosm and the universal
macrocosm; and, finally, *la Littérature de Tout à l'heure* (The
Literature of the Hour), that "Cromwell's Preface to Symbolism," considered at the time the credo of a generation. Its
author, Charles Morice, regarded the "law of Analogy and the
Gospel of Correspondences" as the foundation of all poetry.
Without any precise documentation, it is difficult to ascertain
whether Mallarmé had involuntarily contributed to launching
the vogue or whether it had brought him back to doctrines
that had once attracted him. In any case, a note in 1890 to
V.-E. Michelet, thanking him for his book *L'Ésotérisme dans
l'Art* (Esotericism in Art), indicates his solidarity with the de-
fenders of esotericism: "Occultism is the commentary of pure
signs, which all literature obeys, an immediate leap of the spirit.
Your very convinced. Stéphane Mallarmé."

Still, as always he kept his distance. He would never be compromised in the noisy manifestations that were soon organized around these ideas, such as the famous Rosicrucian "salon" at which a crowd amassed to hear Sâr Péladan's prophecies. Mallarmé was always forearmed against hasty adventures of the mind. And so he remained, as Morice has noted, the *conscience* of the movement, and not its propagandist. "In Art, he is our living conscience, the difficult Master one dreams of contenting."

III. GLORY

There are few examples of such uncontested literary and moral authority. The daily press, of course, continued its incomprehension, mockery, and even violent attacks against the man who had, almost in spite of himself, conquered the public and glory, without ever having made a concession to either. Despite his inalterable modesty, Mallarmé had to recognize that by about 1890 he occupied an exceptional and privileged position in letters. It brought him little else but testimonials and proofs of respect, friendship, and admiration. However, this was most comforting to a man who had so long struggled alone and obscure. Young men came to him for counsel and encouragement: "Your opinion is more precious to me than any other, and I should be happy to submit some very short attempts to you for you to give me your opinion of one of them. It will be definitive to me." So wrote Pierre Louÿs, then a neophyte. It was he who would give his provincial friend, Paul Valéry, then nineteen, "the shock of Mallarmé's work." Less than a month later, Valéry wrote: "Dear Master. A young man lost in the depths of the provinces, whom rare fragments, discovered by chance in reviews, have permitted to guess at and love the secret splendor of your work, dares to introduce himself. . . ." He closed the letter "hoping for counsel in the same writing that, in 'Hérodiade,' dazzles and throws one into despair."

The Master had careful and encouraging words for all. He replied to Valéry: "The gift of subtle analogy with adequate music—you possess that, certainly, which is everything." And André Fontainas said of the note Mallarmé sent on receiving

his book, *le Sang des Fleurs* (The Blood of Flowers), "It was
the origin of my happiness in literature and, perhaps, of my
religion." For all these young men who approached him, for
all the "mardistes," Mallarmé was not only a master and a
friend, he was an exceptional being, the object of a real religion.
Pierre Louÿs wrote the following to Paul Valéry, with no
ironical intent: "Saint Mallarmé said these very words to me
last week: 'But, sir, not only do I approve of you and support
you, but I promise you the succor of all my friends.'" Verlaine
declared to Louÿs, when the latter visited him in the hospital,
that Mallarmé was indisputably the "leader of them all."

Always benevolent and ready to be of service with a discreet
recommendation, he encouraged and aided many. He was
affectionately in attendance at the last moments of his old
friend Villiers, and intervened to try to save Gauguin from
poverty. As in the time of his friendship with Manet, he always
took sides with true literature and authentic art. His acquaint-
ances included Berthe Morisot, Manet's sister-in-law, Renoir,
Odilon Redon, Gauguin, Vuillard, and soon Claude Debussy.
The following lines of Mirbeau dispense with any further
commentary on the prestige he enjoyed with his friends and
their affection for him:

> I have vowed a worship for you, my friend, of which you are
> perhaps ignorant, and which makes me lead a nobler and better
> life. In an hour of discouragement, I think of you; and it is like a
> stroll by the sea. Maeterlinck wrote me this morning and I excerpt
> these words from his letter: ". . . with the exception of Stéphane
> Mallarmé, whom I consider one of the greatest thinkers and loftiest
> spirits in this world . . ." It is true, and he could have added, and
> certainly did add in his heart: "and one of the brightest goodnesses
> of this world." I embrace you tenderly (Letter quoted by Mondor,
> *op. cit.*, p. 590).

Nor should one imagine Mallarmé always absorbed in some
distant dream, or laboriously writing rare, hermetic poems. His
social mien, often relaxed and smiling, never disclosed his
hidden torments.

To his daughter Geneviève, he wrote: "Alone when I work, I
dislike being so at other moments" (July 21, 1891). When the
occasion demanded, how well he knew how to be familiar and

intimate! Geneviève had become his friend and constant companion. If she absented herself from the house, he would send her the least piece of news: "Your lazy Papa writes on this Sunday morning while the workers are repairing the rowboat, which had developed dangerous and secret caries in its old age" (August 8, 1901).

He maintained an enormous correspondence, with precision and exquisite politeness. This poet who always claimed impotency revealed to his friends an astonishing fertility in madrigals and other verse compliments. New Year's gifts, Easter eggs, birthdays and feast days, photographs, fans, albums, and dedications all found him using his agile pen for one of those innumerable quatrains that gave him relaxation from the Great Work and regaled his friends. Long after his death they were grouped under the title *Vers de Circonstance* (Occasional Poems).[4] Even envelopes were covered with verse. In these "Loisirs de la Poste" (Postal Leisures), no less than in other diversions of the same type, that graceful preciosity and mischievous good humor that defined his daily personality flows out in "voluptuous spirals," as Jean Royère has said. Gratuitous games? No doubt, but perhaps these were again "studies with better in view," scales and arpeggios, researches into words, sonorities, and rhythms, and especially into the secret bonds between thought and space, whether the space were a white page, the pleated wing of a fan, the fragile edge of a frame, or even the unassuming rectangle of an envelope. Mallarmé declared that he had discovered an "obvious connection between the ordinary format of envelopes and the disposition of a quatrain."

The same would be true for the form of a fan and the disposition of a sonnet, as in "l'Éventail de Madame Mallarmé" (Mme Mallarmé's Fan). The original was written in red ink on a fan of silver paper decorated with tiny white daisies. It is a grace-

4 Except for those few pieces which he viewed with favor and included in the collection *Poésies complètes:* "Chansons bas" (Soft Songs), "Feuillet d'Album" (Album Leaf), "Petits Airs" (Little Airs), "Éventail" (Fan), "Billet à Whistler" (Note to Whistler), and some charming little poems composed for Méry Laurent ("O si chère de loin . . ." [Oh so dear from far], "Rondels").

ful piece, but in it Mallarmé's preciosity becomes unnecessary complication.[5] The poet again takes up the theme of the analogy fan/wing/verse. He adds the image of a limpid, fictitious mirror, quickened behind the woman by the reflected movement of the object that she holds in her hand. Thus the "futur vers" (future verse) would suggest a potential world, and Mallarmé hopes that in its mute language the fan in the woman's hand may do as much.

And now, in 1890, surrounded by praise and incense, he was suddenly as nervous as a beginner: he was leaving for various cities in Belgium to deliver a series of lectures on Villiers de l'Isle-Adam. Yet his reputation had preceded him; and his attractive voice, limpidly manipulating each sentence, conquered his public, despite the seriousness of his subject and the hermeticism of his style. There was one exception: the baffled colonel in Antwerp who, after a few minutes, noisily left the hall crying, "This man reading that nameless stupidity is either drunk or mad!"

But rare now were those who rose up against what the élite approved. Two events in 1891 confirmed the triumph of the Symbolist movement and its "leader in spite of himself." First was the famous banquet in honor of Moréas' *Pelerin passionné*, organized by the author himself. Barrès and Henri de Régnier asked Mallarmé to preside over this gathering of everyone of importance in the republic of letters. It was much more of a testimonial dinner for Mallarmé than for Moréas, despite the jokes and disorder which reigned over the affair. A month later, Jules Huret's inquiry in *l'Écho de Paris* into France's literary evolution gave young writers the opportunity to present their almost unanimous homage to Mallarmé's influence and authority in poetry. The master used the occasion to clarify his position with regard to the contemporary movement:

> I abominate schools and anything that resembles them. . . . I was made to look like the leader of a school, first by the fact that I have always been interested in the ideas of young people; then, undoubtedly, by my sincerity in recognizing what was new in the contributions of newcomers. For at heart I am solitary. . . .

5 Commentary: Mauron, p. 128. Noulet, p. 465.

He also defined his poetry and showed its relationship with Symbolism:

> To *name* an object is to suppress three-quarters of the enjoyment of a poem, which is made up of gradual guessing: the dream is to *suggest* it. It is the perfect use of that mystery that constitutes the symbol: to evoke an object little by little in order to show a frame of mind, or, conversely, to choose an object and cause a state of mind to emerge from it, through a series of decipherings.

In closing, he said to Jules Huret, "When you come right down to it, the world is made to culminate in a beautiful book." Was this not the goal of his entire life? And yet, despite his several editions: the beautiful pamphlet of the "Faune" in 1875; the photolithographed volume of his poems in 1887; *Tiroir de Laque* (Lacquered Drawer), which appeared in 1891 under the more neutral title of *Pages* and contained the majority of his prose works—the Book of which he had been dreaming for twenty years had not yet seen the light. At that moment of triumph for the poet and the movement he had stimulated, no one dared to decide whether it was overweening ambition or insurmountable impotency. . . . As for Mallarmé, he had his eyes fixed on the future and had not yet given up.

9 · Into Himself

Tel qu'en Lui-même enfin l'éternité le change,
Le Poète suscite avec un glaive nu
Son siècle épouvanté de n'avoir pas connu
Que la mort triomphait dans cette voix étrange!
"LE TOMBEAU D'EDGAR POE"

(As into Himself eternity finally changes him,
The Poet arouses with a naked sword
His century horrified not to have known
That death was triumphing in that strange voice!)

I. THE MAN OF LETTERS

This was certainly glory with all its obligations: new works sent by disciples and confreres, requiring thanks with pertinent remarks; contributions which took precious time from the essential; and even more, perhaps, "honors": manifestations, commemorations, meetings of all kinds, which must be attended if not presided over. Mallarmé hid whenever he could. But more often, through courtesy or lassitude, or perhaps because this "solitary" did not detest the world and the conversation of intelligent men, he accepted. The famous banquets of *La Plume* (The Pen), which periodically brought together a hundred or so literary people, were twice chaired by Mallarmé. It was at the meeting of February, 1893, that he pronounced, in the guise of a toast, his "Salut" (Salutation), the poem with which he later introduced his volume of poems, no doubt to stun the reader:

Rien, cette écume, vierge vers
À ne désigner que la coupe . . .

(Nothing, this foam, virgin verse
Denoting only the cup . . .) [1]

Here again, as in so many other occasional pieces, a simple word, a concrete and familiar image, is the root of an interplay

[1] Commentary: Thibaudet, p. 311. Noulet, p. 467. Mauron, p. 99. Gengoux, p. 107. G. Davies, in *Les Lettres*, III, Nos. 9, 10, 11, p. 194. Wais, p. 548. Chassé, *Lueurs*, p. 103.

between metaphorical superimpressions. "This foam," this nothing, these champagne bubbles, awaken in the poet's imagination a seascape and a vision of sirens who seem to be drowning because they are viewed upside down as indistinct forms at the bottom of the goblet. Mallarmé and those surrounding him become the Argonauts on an adventure, a difficult ocean voyage. They are in the prow, knifing through the waves, and he is already at the stern, but standing upright, despite the euphoria of the wine and the pitching of the ship. Standing there, he proposes a toast to everything that brings them together tonight, sorrows and hopes: "Solitude, récif, étoile" (Solitude, reefs, star).

Thus, after twenty years, oceanic and cosmic imagery had found its way back into Mallarmé's poetry. Here it would seem to be inconsequential, slipped into an unimportant occasional piece beginning with the word "nothing" and apparently unpretentious, a few lines as effervescent as champagne. Yet the essential metaphor at its center warns us to go further. This ship is literature, its sail is the white canvas, i.e., the white page, and this nothing, this "foam," is poetry, "virgin verse," nothingness in an empty cup.[2] The images of nothingness, poetry, and the sea were joined here for the first time. It was not to be the last.

There had indeed been many reefs on the endless voyage. The least painful were the incomprehension and the jeering. More cruel were the silence, the susceptibility, the wounded vanity, the jealousy, and other pettinesses of others. Worst was the day-to-day struggle for existence, which had prematurely worn the poet down: perpetual money worries and what he called his "forced labor": the job of teaching, which he had never really liked. For thirty years it had always paralyzed his vocation, daily stealing the best hours from his true work. Only the nights were his, and gradually Mallarmé stopped sleeping. He had literally not slept for ten years. "I am awake twenty-four

---

2 This is a double pun. Mallarmé plays both on the word "coupe" (a drinking cup and a pause in a line of verse) and the homonyms "vers-verre" (verse-glass). Chassé admits only one of these meanings (caesura and verse), and yet all the rather precious ingenuity of the sonnet lies in this play on words.

hours a day," he wrote to the astonished J. H. Rosny. Imagine, an "absolute insomnia," omnipresent and creating an almost inhuman way of life!

This no doubt explains how Mallarmé was able to assume such a prodigious variety of tasks; not only his classes and the tasks they carried with them but the innumerable obligations of a man of letters: correspondence, inquiries, proofreading. He had finally decided to make excerpts of his work available to the public in a book entitled *Vers et Prose*, to be published by Perrin. At the same time he was preparing a new edition of *Vathek*. And of course there could be no question of sacrificing the traditional Tuesdays. Yet he still managed to meditate, to stuff his drawers with the bits of paper that so intrigued his following, and, more than ever before, to circulate couplets and quatrains all around him. Méry Laurent urged him to look over and rewrite, if necessary, the *Contes et Légendes de l'Inde ancienne* (Tales and Legends of Ancient India), published fifteen years earlier by Mary Dummer. In Germany, Stefan George requested a contribution to his *Blätter für die Kunst* (Pages on Art), and the *National Observer* in London asked for a series of articles. If only he could resign himself to writing like everyone else! But no; he declared one day to Camille Mauclair,

> How many times have I resolved to write the books I was carry-ing in my head, contenting myself with a normal French style, more or less eloquent and expressive, with the customary rhythms and syntax, vowing to myself that I would shake off the yoke; and then, at the moment I began, I would know that I could not, that one has no right so to misuse the written form; and I would begin to study what it requires (Camille Mauclair, *L'Art en silence* [Art in Silence]).

Trapped by his own decisions and enslaved by an exigency that has no equivalent in modern literature, he had only one hope of achieving his Work: to escape his "forced labor." A pension at fifty would make it possible for him to live. In a letter to Coppée asking for intervention on his behalf, he wrote: "School has become brutal for me. I am going to take the bull by the horns; and I am going to withdraw a small sum that has been hard-earned." Coppée evidently had some influence, and the much-desired deliverance occurred on October, 1893. Mallarmé obtained his pension. He could now devote himself at last to his Work.

II. MALLARMÉ'S RELIGION

Finally liberated—or at least, so he thought—from bondage, Mallarmé turned with confidence to the future. What was the nature of his meditations and plans? A brief backward glance will help to establish the state of Mallarmé's thought at this point in his career, thought that would henceforth be hidden with more and more minute care in the folds of a sibylline style.

1. At twenty-four, as we have seen, Mallarmé had discovered his "religion." Paradoxical on the surface, it seemed both to exclude God and to affirm his belief in something "divine." Beyond the daily world of contingency, chance, and illusion, he had in fact discovered the existence of a higher world, a "spiritual universe" with "a logical constitution," which he called Beauty. Guy Delfel has summarized this "esthetic religion" in this pertinent statement: "The transcendental aspect of the real is not a person, but a Cosmos organized under the sign of Beauty." Mallarmé seems to have remained faithful to that religion, as more than one text shows, e.g., "Prose pour des Esseintes," his reply to René Ghil: "One cannot do without Eden," and the lecture, "Music and Letters," which he gave at Oxford and Cambridge in 1892: "If a religious resurgence is to spring up in France in the future, it will be the joyful amplification of the heaven-instinct in everyone." Perhaps, as E. Fraenkel feels (*Perspectives sur Mallarmé*), such remarks indicate the persistence of an unavowed hope in the depths of his soul.

2. Be that as it may, Mallarmé's religion was not pure abstraction. It was certainly *metaphysical* to the extent that it represented for him a science of the divine, but it was *mystical* in its postulation of an accessible but mysterious reality, to be "enjoyed privately." However, one must beware of words: the enjoyment remained intellectual. It was the emotion of an idea, and it consisted of embracing the spiritual universe and penetrating its mystery. This mystery was in no way irreducible, but seemed so because it could be reached only by certain means. Mallarmé's religion is characterized by the "ascesis" it

requires to pass from the daily world to the spiritual universe,
the "duty" spoken of in "Toast funèbre" and "Prose":

> . . . *le devoir*
> *Idéal que nous font les jardins de cet astre . . .*

> > (. . . the ideal duty
> > Set for us by the gardens of this star . . .)

And only poetry can accomplish this ascesis. Mallarmé repeated
this once more in the Cambridge lecture: "To catch the world's
mystery habitually by surprise, to identify it, strikes me as an
obligation of anyone who would unleash the Infinite." In the
last analysis, this esthetic religion is a *religion of poetry.*

3. The poet is consecrated because he alone has the power to
discover and suggest the spiritual world to others, through his
intuitions of the mysterious analogies that bind that world to
ours. As he declared to Léo d'Orfer in 1884, only the poet
confers meaning on existence. His sole duty is the "orphic
explanation of the Earth," the recreation on the plane of art of
the Beauty hidden at the heart of things. Thus, for the first time
in French literature, from a means of expression poetry became
with Mallarmé a means of discovery and, as has since been
said, a "spiritual experience" which confers a religious character on the poet. He is consecrated because he is the celebrant
of an office in which other men are invited to commune with
him. "Poetry, annointment": these simple words, which appear
in a "divagation" of 1895, "L'Action restreinte" (Restrained
Action), summarize Mallarmé's religion.

4. For thirty years the world had been an immense enigma to
decipher. He had to learn to read the "play inscribed in the
folio of the sky." Hence his interest in the doctrines that come
under the vague and general name of occultism. They represented the effort of all ages to discover the structure of the
cosmos and define its hidden relationships. He had no criticism
of the postulates on which these doctrines were founded. They
had long been his own. He did criticize their gratuitousness, in
that they seemed to remain on a speculative plane, while for
him, the poet, the only valuable discoveries were made through
creation. These reservations had been only recently formulated:
"Anyone who blindly splits this art in two, or separates off the

[margin handwritten note: MALLARMÉ AS PRIEST]

delicious, modest, and yet expressible metaphors to realize them in another magic, does wrong" ("Magie" [Magic]). He returned to this distinction in January, 1895, protesting against "easy occultism with its inscrutable ecstasies" and approving "poetry, close to the idea, music par excellence."

He rediscovered his poetic experiences through the fundamentals common to all these traditions: first, the basic idea that the original Nothingness contains everything potentially, beginning with the polarity of Being, the source of all contradictions, mingled in it at the outset. From that very polarity, Life is born, by its very nature vibration and alternation, i.e., rhythm, in both the universe-macrocosm and man-microcosm. "As for me, as a man of letters I rejoice otherwise. In the mind of whoever has dreamed of human beings up to himself, there exists only an exact tally of purely rhythmical motifs of being, which are its recognizable signs: it is my pleasure to decipher them everywhere" (*Notes sur le Théâtre* [Theater Notes], 1887). The fundamental rhythm of life is cyclical and breaks down into four beats, or seasons. Mallarmé spoke the same year of the theatrical Mystery as a "multiple tetrology, paralleling a returning cycle of years." These are in turn multiplied again as if in mirrors, according to the principle of analogy which establishes infinite relationships among all things. Hence contraries are reabsorbed into one another and multiplicity is resolved into unity, the quintessence of everything. "What genius it takes to be a poet! What a lightning of instinct simply to enclose life, virgin in its synthesis and illuminating everything!"

5. But deciphering the world is not enough. To be a poet, one must also recreate it. More precisely, only in recreating the world through metaphor does one succeed in deciphering it. That "lightning of instinct" and the demon of analogy lead the poet to consummate the supreme Act, "to throw the dice in the night" and fix Infinity in his Work, that true condensation of the entire universe, not by description but by suggestion. As he once said to Huret: "To *name* an object is to suppress three-quarters of the enjoyment of a poem, which is made up of gradual guessing: the dream is to *suggest* it." Only suggestion permits the passage from one world to the other. "I call this aim Transposition; Structure is something else" ("Crise de vers"

[The Crisis of Poetry]).[3] Such a transposition is the domain of
poetry, in contrast to "commercial" prose. Poetry is the Magic
which must dispense its charms and spells to bring forth another
world: "To evoke, in a deliberate shadow, the stilled object,
by allusive, never direct words that come down to an equivalent
silence, constitutes the nearest approach to creating."

In this alchemy, the poet's every effort must tend to make the
object disappear in favor of the Idea, as in "Prose pour des
Esseintes," and as in music. Mallarmé never sat at a concert
"without perceiving in the midst of that obscure sublimity a
rough draft, in its original state, of one of those poems immanent in humanity." Because of the very nature of music, this
could only be a sketch forever inadequate to its object. By contrast, poetry is the "art of achieving the transposition of the
symphony to the Book. . . . For it is undeniably not from the
elementary sonorities of brasses, strings, and woodwinds, but
from the intellectual word at its apogee that music results,
plenteously and clearly, as the sum of the relationships existing
among all things" ("Crise de vers").

6. Mallarmé had thought for years that the best poetic form
in which to fix this ensemble of relationships was the drama,
the only one capable of summing up the very drama of the
world and consummating, for and before an entire people, the
"unique act." At this point, despite the unquestioned success
of a certain kind of theater which he had to some extent inspired, notably that of Maeterlinck, whose advent he himself
had celebrated,[4] he returned to his original conception: the
Book, the "grimoire," that he had described to Verlaine in
"Autobiographie" as "architectural and premeditated." For
"everything in the world exists to culminate in a book" ("Le
Livre, instrument spirituel." Mallarmé's hard-won leisure would
be devoted to creating this book, as well as to clarifying his concept of it.

3 "Crise de vers" was first published as an article in the *National
Observer*.
4 It is said that in 1889 Mirbeau wrote his famous article about *la
Princesse Maleine*, in which he compares Maeterlinck to Shakespeare, at
Mallarmé's instigation.

III. VARIATIONS ON A SUBJECT

Mallarmé's fidelity to regular lines of verse and to fixed forms—sonnets, rondels—might give the impression that he was indifferent to the revolution in form that had been taking place for several years and with which he had been closely associated, at least as a witness. This is evidently not so. He only wanted time to reflect before drawing his own conclusions.

The first echo of these reflections appeared in 1892 in his British lecture, "La Musique et les Lettres" (Music and Letters):

Indeed, I bring news. Most surprising. Nothing like it has been seen before.
We have made contact with the line of verse.

In seeking to break the rhythm of the line "according to a more complex thyrsos," by playing with hidden timbres and rhymes, poets like Baudelaire and Rimbaud had already created prose poems. Even more recently, free verse had been invented. This transformation, "unexpectedly prepared underneath and in advance by Verlaine," began internally with a relaxation of the "rigid and puerile mechanism" of the alexandrine ("Crise de vers"). Following Verlaine's example, poets like Jules Laforgue and Henri de Régnier used the 11- or 13-syllable line, initiating the public into the "sure charm of irregular verse" ("au charme certain du vers faux"). Finally came the dissolution of an official number of syllables, i.e., actual free verse. Mallarmé did not think that the orthodox line would disappear: that "great general and secular pipe-organ" would continue to be heard on important occasions. Nevertheless, he recognized that "for the first time in the literary history of a people, a lofty and most new liberty" had been acquired. Free verse, he said, is an individual modulation allowing the poet to translate his internal melody; for "each soul is a melody to be reassembled; each one's flute or viola is for that purpose."

But he did see signs of a more profound unease in this "crisis of poetry." "Literature is here undergoing an exquisite, a fundamental crisis." For the first time, the very value of literature was

being questioned, in itself and in terms of the other arts, especially music. If it is true that the mind "has to do with nothing
else than the musicality of everything," then literature might
risk dilution through orientation toward evocation and suggestion. But Mallarmé sees in this only the undisputed supremacy
of literature, which does not have to meet with music, because
"since Wagner, music has met with verse to form Poetry." For
"Music and Letters are alternative faces, the one welcoming
darkness, the other sparkling with certitude, of one, the only
Phenomenon: I call it the Idea" ("La Musique et les Lettres").

His increasing meditations on "Letters," as he was right to
call them, gave rise to a series of articles in the *Revue Blanche*
in 1895 and 1896: "Variations sur un sujet" (Variations on a
Subject). The subject is still the same: the Book. The two
essential articles are "Le Livre, instrument spirituel" and "Le
Mystère dans les Lettres" (Mystery in Letters). The final stage
of his thought can be clarified through these and other texts
of the same period.

1. The Book has a certain number of particular properties
which ordinarily pass unnoticed. First, it is made up of a
unique material: the alphabet. Following is a highly important
fragment from an article outline written in 1893:

> By means of its twenty-four signs, as well as by means of multiple
> fusions within the sentence and then the line of verse, a system
> arranged like a spiritual zodiac, this literature so exactly called
> Letters implies its doctrine, which is as special, abstract, and esoteric
> as a theology. This is simply because some concepts are of such a
> nature, or of so rarefied and ordinarily unreachable a nature, that
> for expression they require special and supreme means, whose num-
> ber, like theirs, is not unlimited (*Oeuvres complètes*, p. 850).

As we know, Mallarmé had always dreamed of reconstituting
the original, universal language, in which every sound would
recover its own essential value. In 1869 he noted: "Such a sound
signifies *this* par excellence." *Les Mots anglais* had tried to
point out such meanings for at least certain sounds. Since then,
he had continued to meditate on the value of each letter and
had attempted to apply the results of these meditations in his
verse, to such an extent that tables have been constructed of
these expressive and symbolic values (Scherer, *op. cit.*, pp. 25 ff.,

and especially R. G. Kohn, *op. cit.*, pp. 98 ff.). In fact, the obsessive recurrence of some of Mallarmé's key images seems to have been dictated by their vowel or consonant quality, e.g., the piercing luminosity of the "i" in the words "Midi" and "pierreries," or in the sonnet of the swan; the disturbing sharpness of the "u" in "plume," "Pénultième," "chute," "sépulcre"; the ample, rounded resonance of the "o" in "sonore," "mandore," "hyperbole," "symbole"; the negative quality of the "n" in "nul," "nu," "néant," "nuit," "neige"; or the winged, feminine feeling of the "v" in "vierge," "vase," "vol," or "éventail." [5]

This could even be one of the principal reasons for the narrowness of Mallarmé's lexicon. After sorting, the poet retained only those words which had a form that seemed to him to have preserved the most affinities to their primordial meaning. In any case, this is the secret of that magic with which Mallarmé wished to invest the poet, that "enchanter of letters," as he called him; and it is what, in fact, makes his own poetry so disturbing.

2. From the above, it is easier to understand what he meant by the statement in his letter to Coppée in 1866: "In a poem the words are reflected one upon the other." "Crise de vers" in 1892 repeated and clarified the formula: "They are lit up by mutual reflections like a virtual trail of fire on precious stones." These lines of the "Mystère dans les lettres" (1896) indicate its final form:

Words by themselves burst into a many-faceted flame, recognized as the rarest or most worthwhile for the mind, center of vibratory suspense; which perceives them independently of their ordinary order, projected as on the inner surface of a grotto, while their mobility or principle lasts, this being what cannot be said about speech: all eager, before extinction, for a reciprocity of distant flames or one presented on the bias like a contingency.

The word, then, is a jewel of which each letter constitutes a facet. It is also the element of a superior unity: the line of verse

[5] Certainly similar preoccupations are to be found in literature before Mallarmé, notably in the poets of Art for Art's Sake and the Parnassians. But what distinguishes Mallarmé is that he went back to the sources of poetic language to seek not only the expressive value of phonemes but also their mystical value.

or the sentence, themselves elements of the supreme unity
which is "the Book, total expression of the letter."

3. One of his last discoveries was that the Book constitutes a
three-dimensional *volume*. In other words, literature is not only
music, but also, and perhaps above all, an art of space. In this
light, the measure of unity for the book is no longer the word,
or even the line of verse, but the *page*, on which each element
must take the place assigned it in a spatial ensemble:

> From time immemorial, the poet has known the place of this
> line in the sonnet, which is inscribed for the pure mind or on pure
> space. In my turn, if I cannot, knowledgeably, imagine a particular
> motif at a special point, as to both page and height, oriented to
> its own or to the work's light, I misunderstand the volume and the
> marvel which its structure intimates ("le Livre, instrument spir-
> ituel," *Oeuvres complètes*, p. 380).

The work is, then, created progressively, emerging gradually from nothingness, in function of, and out of, empty white
space, the materialization of silence. Music is thus reintegrated
into literature, because every subject implies "an agreement as
to its corresponding place in the volume." Everything then becomes "suspense, the disposition on the white pages of alter-
nating and contrasting fragments collaborating toward the total
rhythm, which would be the stilled poem." Therefore, there is
"nothing fortuitous" in a literary work, which is decidedly
"chance vanquished word by word." Whence this amazing idea,
which he would shortly later attempt to apply:

> Why should not a strong freshet of grandeur, thought or emo-
> tion, a continued sentence in large type, one line to a page, in gradu-
> ated positions, keep the reader in top form throughout the book,
> appealing to the power of his enthusiasm: with, all around, tiny
> secondary groups in order of their importance, explanatory or deriva-
> tive—a scattering of ornaments (*ibid.*, p. 381).

4. Finally, the formation of the book as a thick packet, which
makes it a "minuscule tomb for the soul," and the folding of the
pages, in which Mallarmé finds a religious value, seem to shut
the book on a secret. This secret is the world's drama in all its
mystery. Like the fan, the book, as Mallarmé so magnificently
said, is "like a gathered-up flight ready to take to the open, . . .

the hymn, harmony and joy, like a pure ensemble grouped in some lightning circumstance, of the relations among all things." Only one kind of man would be capable of writing such a book, the one described in a passage which R. G. Kohn has pointed out as vitally important:

. . . [one who] recreated by himself has taken care strictly to preserve from what he has discarded a reverence for the twenty-four letters as they are fixed, through the miracle of infinity, in whatever language is his; then a sense of their symmetries, action, reflections, up to a transfiguration into supernatural terms, which is verse; this civilized man of Eden possesses, above all other goods, the element of felicities, a doctrine as well as a country. When its initiative, or the potential force of the divine letters teaches him to put them to use ("la Musique et les Lettres").

To catch the great rhythms of the universe, notably the quadruple rhythm of the seasons, to understand the symbolic meaning of the twenty-four letters of the alphabet, that "spiritual zodiac," and know how to put them to use in a book: how could a poet who attempted such an ideal fail to be accused of unintelligibility? Certainly, everything written should present an external meaning, even an indifferent one, if only to turn away the dabbler, "charmed that, at first reading, nothing in it concerns him." But it should also comprise "a kind of mirroring" underneath, an "air or chant under the text," which might lead the reader's imagination through the work and suggest its real meaning. Is this a case of mystification? Mallarmé was content to reply, in "le Mystère dans les Lettres," to all his detractors, with this simple sentence: "I prefer, in the face of aggression, to retort that some of my contemporaries do not know how to read." No fuss—there are simply those who can and those who cannot read.

Thus, Mallarmé had not given this series of articles a hermetic appearance in a desire to be provocative. He felt that it was impossible to be false to himself in the very statement of his own ideas. If he introduced unusual typographical artifices in the exposé—breaks in the text, white spaces, etc.—it was because he was seeking a new formula midway between ordinary prose and the prose poem, which he would have liked to call a

"critical poem." He would later explain this in the bibliographical notes accompanying these articles when they were published in book form as *Divagations:*

> To mobilize the diverse lights of the mind around an idea, at the
> distance willed, by sentences. . . . No doubt there is a means there,
> for a poet who does not habitually practice free verse, to show, in
> the guise of comprehensive and brief pieces, eventually, with ex-
> perience, those immediate rhythms of thought that govern a prosody
> (*Oeuvres complètes*, p. 1576).

We are alerted. In approaching Mallarmé's work in his "last
manner," we must seek the apparent, logical meaning; we must
even find it rigorously maintained throughout, through and in
spite of that "enlarged syntax" that he refined by use. But *this
is not enough.* In clinging to an external interpretation, we run
the risk of impoverishing the content of the work. His work
requires a tireless rereading, with attention to the sonorities
and all the many possible meanings of each word, as well as to
the infinite resonances of the whole. We must bear ourselves
toward it as toward a drawing which suggests many images
through the interplay of line and contour; allowing the formation within us of the diverse impressions that are superimposed
one upon the other and give the poem its full breadth and
wealth. A thankless task at first, but well worth the effort, for
to the reader who goes faithfully to the end it makes available
an enjoyment of art and thought to be found in no other body
of works.

IV. THE HERMIT OF VALVINS

Retirement from teaching did not cause Mallarmé to renounce the Parisian life of the reluctant man of letters that he
had become. On the contrary, the "profession" had never before
so absorbed him. His unfailing courtesy forbade him to refuse
any invitation, and he made it his scrupulous duty to answer
every letter and acknowledge every book sent to him. All
through the winter there were toasts, correspondence, letters of
recommendation, and notes of thanks. His position in the
avant garde included him in every survey or poll. He was inter-
viewed about everything and everybody: Voltaire, Poe, Tolstoy,
Verlaine (who had just died), Marceline Desbordes-Valmore,

Maupassant; Scandinavian literature, theater, graphology; springtime, cats, feminine bicycle outfits, top hats, the ideals of a twenty-year-old. Indefatigably he gave a personal opinion on everything and managed to coin an unexpected phrase each time. Apropos of the bicycle:

To design, exactly, requires that the artisan be as oblivious to custom as he is to useless ornament—only the direct execution of the idea, as the object is presented, in order to please and be useful, causing a completely modern impression of truth ("Sur le Beau et l'Utile" [On the Beautiful and Useful], *Oeuvres complètes*, p. 880).

On the subject of hats:

From the fact that at one human date they were put on heads, they will always be there. Whoever has put the like of them on once cannot take them off. The world will end, not the hat; probably it has existed from all time in an invisible state ("Sur le chapeau haut de forme" [On the Top Hat], *Oeuvres complètes*, p. 881).

Each new banquet heard a toast to some friend, in prose or in verse: to Catulle Mendès, Gustave Kahn, Verhaeren, Jean Moréas ("the first to make a meal the consequence of a book of verse"). Upon the death of Verlaine in 1896, he was elected "Prince of Poets." Requests for contributions came from everywhere. Each time, he wrote a few lines or exhumed a forgotten piece from a desk drawer: "Hommage" to Puvis de Chavannes, "Remémoration" to Belgian friends. In 1897, Vielé-Griffin and Paul Valéry had the idea of bringing together for a dinner some ten or twelve of the faithful from the "Tuesdays." Immediately the uninvited protested. Catulle Mendès and Rodenbach were offended, and discord soon entered the camp of Mallarmé's closest friends.

To tell the truth, it had been in the air for some time. The Master's affability, detachment, and loyalty could not prevent tender feelings, jealousy, and tactlessness. And his fame was too great not to excite envy. The attacks against him doubled— against him who had never accepted any compromise. An alumnus of the Tuesdays, Adolphe Retté, distilled his venom in *la Plume:* he described the works of his former master as "monsters characteristic of a moment of literary aberration" and added: "Monsieur Mallarmé knows nothing but mumbo-jumbo." Fortunately, Mallarmé's true friends were at hand. André Gide soon replied in the *Mercure de France:* "I do not reproach Monsieur Retté for his lack of comprehension, but for his insults to someone who deserves *at least* the esteem of those who are not capable of admiring him" (February, 1897).

Mallarmé's publication of *Divagations* in 1897—in self-defense, he said—grouping the majority of his articles and prose poems, drew new attacks as well as protestations of friendship and admiration. A well-placed critic, Chantavoine, decreed in the *Correspondant:* "I have read these ramblings; they plunged me into madness." Pierre Louÿs, however, sent Mallarmé these enthusiastic words: "Your book has produced an enormous effect on me. It seems to me that in a future that we cannot imagine, reference will be made to it in order to fix the boundaries of human reverie, and, better yet, its eternal laws" (quoted in Mondor, *op. cit.,* p. 750).

No, he had not abandoned the life of a man of letters. But after a few weeks in Paris, his thoughts turned constantly back to his beloved Valvins, where he could at least work and meditate, far from disputes and cliques. Valvins! where he went before the spring, shivering, with his cat Lilith; where, in the summer, there would be calm boat rides with one or another of his real friends or disciples: Henri de Régnier, Paul Valéry, Léopold Dauphin.

Was it perhaps the influence of a rather melancholy landscape? or the periodic return of certain ailments that, although he was still well under sixty, sometimes gave rise to anxiety about the completion of his Work? or the very course of his meditations, which, after the decade or so that might be called the "precious period," was bringing him back now in a cycle to the time of "Igitur"? In any case, his thoughts turned more and more toward death.

In 1893 he wrote a "Tombeau" for a projected monument to Baudelaire. It was not published until two years later, when it sowed immediate confusion among the ranks of the "Mallarmistes." The diverse play of images was in fact far from being in the best of taste, although it was admirably suited to the morbid religiosity of the poet of "Tableaux parisiens" (Parisian Tableaux).[6] To evoke Baudelaire, Mallarmé calls up the glow of a street lamp with a yawning sewer at its base. But he also immediately imagines the ruins of a buried temple under the sidewalk, expelling torrents of rubies and mud from a gaping crack caused by an excavation. Among the rubies stands a grimacing statue of Anubis, God of death, an idol with a glittering snout. The idol—a still imperfect symbol of Baudelaire's poetry —is soon replaced, in the flickering gaslight, by the huckstering, shameless form of a prostitute. Is it not the very shade of the poet that is thus evoked, absent and intangible under its funeral veils, a "poison tutélaire" (guardian poison), a troubling perfume which we cannot help breathing in, even though it means that we perish?

Death had come to many of the poets of Mallarmé's generation. Particularly moving was the death of Verlaine in January, 1896. A year later Mallarmé spoke these words at the grave of his old companion-in-arms:

We know that Verlaine is smiling at sharing the immortality of France's greatest poets, with, for example, La Fontaine and Lamartine. His luminous ascent did not last a year; even insult was not lacking; it is useful for a more rapid riddance of the unhappiness inherent to genius—let us only have some regrets for those who assume this function. Before the dear shade departs from here for less severe gardens, let us tenderly hear some friendly words supporting him as they once did: his shade will then be less frightened to follow us to his glory (*Oeuvres complètes*, p. 865).

This is very nearly a short paraphrase of the "Tombeau" published in the *Revue Blanche* at that time, one of his most moving poems in its translucent obscurity and inner vibration:

Verlaine? *il est caché parmi l'herbe, Verlaine* . . .

(Verlaine? he is hidden among the blades of grass . . .)

Before this modest tomb in the Batignolles Cemetery, half swallowed up in the grass swept by the wintry wind, but proud of the remains it sheltered, this "black rock angered by the un-

6 Commentary: Thibaudet, p. 308. Noulet, p. 470. Mauron, p. 171. Gengoux, p. 89. Davies, p. 164. Chassé, *Revue des Sciences humaines*, December, 1951.

settling breeze," could one find more perfectly suited sonorities
to evoke the poet of *Romances sans paroles* (Romances without
Words) and *Sagesse* (Wisdom)? It is a sonnet of flight, the
ungraspable "immaterial mourning." Among the blades of
grass, the clouds, the dead branches where doves coo, one dis-
cerns a discreet presence, something like the murmur of a
narrow, shallow stream: it is death, as close and familiar as
Verlaine's poetry. There are no superimpressions here: a pure
melody is exhaled like a breath. Once certain syntactical pecu-
liarities are grasped ("ni" used in the sense of "not even," 'à ne
surprendre que" for "occupied only in discovering," and the
whole thirteenth line taken as a sort of complement), the
reader can understand and enjoy the poem by recalling any one
of its phrases.

> *La montée lumineuse n'a pas duré un an* . . .

> (The luminous ascent did not last a year . . .)

The poem says: the star of tomorrow has already risen for
Verlaine, but despite the pious hands lingering on his grave-
stone to find the trace and symbol of human troubles on the
somber block, the poet is still not understood. Many a nubile
(in the etymological sense) fold, many a cloud of injustice still
dims his glory. Why then seek him in the externals of his
vagabond life? The true Verlaine is here, hidden in the grass,
where death has changed him, like Poe, "tel qu'en lui-même,"
into his real self. He has only had to wet his lips with death and
hold his breath to be able, naïvely in agreement, to accept it
gently as the donor of glory and immortality.

The cycle was coming fully around. After thirty years, Mallarmé announced:

> I am going to finish "Hérodiade" before the fall: I shall publish
> the Prelude and the Finale in the *Revue Blanche*. It is absolutely
> necessary, so that the collection of my poems will not seem to
> everyone to be incomplete and truncated, . . . to find a way to
> include the poem in its complete form (to Denan, July 21, 1896).

This was not the only reason for turning backwards. He had
renewed his old meditations and was trying to get a new hold
on the curve of his thought in order to close the cycle. He had

covered much ground. A draft fragment of that period shows the poet coming to grips with the absolute through laboriously colliding images:

> *Le fantôme accoudé du pâle écho latent*
> *Sous un voile debout ne dissimule tant*
> *Supérieurement à de noirs plis prophète*
> *Toujours que de ne pas perpétuer du faîte*
> *Divers rapprochements scintillés absolus . . .*

> (The leaning phantom of the latent pale echo
> Standing veiled does not dissimulate so
> Superiorly in dark folds, prophet,
> Forever as not to perpetuate from the pinnacle
> Diverse scintillating and absolute confrontations . . .) [7]

Among the attempts to finish the old poem, only the "Cantique de St. Jean" (Canticle of Saint John) ever saw the light.[8] In a striking metaphor, he describes at once the path of the sun and the hyperbolic flight of the saint's head at the moment of decapitation. This new symbol of the poet transfigured by death rises in an implacably victorious rhythm to the place of eternal cold which is also the place of baptism. It illuminates him, for there he meets with the "Principle that has elected him," i.e., Nothingness—or the Absolute.

Sky, ocean, stars in the night: the décor of "Toast funèbre" seems to be haunting the poet once again. However, it is not possible to be certain of this if one judges solely by the enigmatic piece that appeared only after the author's death, with its feeble "sourire du pâle Vasco" (smile of the pale Vasco), "Au seul souci de voyager" (To the single desire to travel).[9] This fourteen-line poem is not dated, and it is very possible that the idea at least was contemporary to "Le vierge, le vivace, et le bel aujourd'hui." In any case, the "salutation" is in Mallarmé's last

7 The passage is extraordinarily obscure, even for Mallarmé. If *faîte* here means "pinnacle" (of a mountain) it perhaps has a connection with the *pâle écho*. The general meaning of these metaphors seems to be as follows: "Even if we do not have direct and obvious proof of the existence of the absolute, comparable to the echo that might resound from a mountainside, we occasionally glimpse the peak which shows that the mountain is there." *Translators.*

8 Commentary: Mauron, p. 110. Noulet, p. 485. Gengoux, p. 117.

9 Commentary: Mauron, p. 183.

manner, as are certain images: the poop, revels, foam. Rarely did Mallarmé's art of superimpression attain the perfection and suggestive power of this poem. The vision of a ship, its main-yard plunging into a sea white with foam, the foam confused with a bird announcing some buried treasure, finally gives rise to the image of the navigator himself, his smile paled by time. This symbolic vision once again suggests the adventure of the poet, who has been able to glimpse in the night a marvelous bearing for the ship to take; but whose desperate call cannot make the human caravel deviate from its route.

The same décor, less sunny and more grandiosely despairing, appears in the hermetic sonnet that Mallarmé published in a German review in 1895, "A la nue accablante tu" (In the crushing cloud silenced).[10] It is a kind of condensed version of the great cosmic poem which came out two years later. All the poet's obsessions swarm pell-mell around the verb "abolir" (abolish): cloud, sepulcher, foam, hair, siren. The poem is a vague vision arising from a seascape. The sea is unleashed under a low, black sky. He asks, what sepulchral shipwreck "tu" (silenced) by a trumpet unable to dominate the waves' uproar, i.e., unnoticed by the sky itself ("la nue accablante") can have taken place? Abolishing what single and final flotsam, a mast stripped of its sails, what poetic shipwreck has occurred? The yawning abyss, furious at not having swallowed a real ship ("furibond faute / De quelque perdition haute" [furious at the lack / of some lofty loss]), had perhaps drowned nothing more than a fragile dream, a white hair dragging like a hemline of the foam, that chimerical child born from the side of a siren.

The "Coup de Dés" (Throw of the Dice) would go further in carrying the unleashed ocean's roar as far as the stars. But the essence of the drama is summed up and, so to speak, condensed in these fourteen lines. The clashing words and sonorities and the fracas of the "a's" and "u's", the "f's" and explosive consonants, are engraved on the reader's ear and mind and create an extraordinarily haunting effect.

In that same year of 1895, *le Figaro* ran a survey discussion of free verse and published a more restrained piece that the author claimed to have written as a "game." Yet its subtle

10 Commentary: Noulet, p. 475.

arabesque summarizes all of Mallarme's concepts in a supreme Art of Poetry. "Toute l'âme résumée" (The whole soul summed up) [11] revolves around a very simple metaphor. At the sight of rising smoke rings seeming to abolish one another, Mallarmé *imagines* the cigar which skillfully accomplishes a kind of alchemistic operation with each puff:

> *. . . la cendre se sépare*
> *De son clair baiser de feu*
>
> (. . . the ash is separated
> From its bright kiss of fire)

The poet operates in this way, skillfully separating the bright fire of the soul from the ashes of reality.[12] "Ainsi le choeur des romances" (Thus the choir of romances) is separated from vile reality and takes wing on the lips of the divine singer. Mallarmé concluded with a couplet in which a definition of Symbolism could be deciphered, were it not that such an interpretation would deprive the couplet of its essential meaning by making it mean merely the vague song of the Decadents:

> *Le sens trop précis rature*
> *Ta vague littérature.*
>
> (Meaning too precise ruins
> Your vague literature.)

But, as he pointed out himself with regard to his fourteen-line poems, as distinguished from the sonnets, the entire poem and not just the last two lines contains the essential. Here the bright kiss of fire "résume" (sums up) Mallarmé's doctrine and the poet's soul.

v. "un coup de dés"

In May, 1897, the international review *Cosmopolis* published a strange and esoteric work. Its seven hundred and some words

11 Commentary: Mauron, p. 181. Noulet, p. 488; II, p. 140. Gengoux, p. 105. Wais, p. 504. Chassé, *Revue de l'Histoire littéraire de la France,* July, 1952, p. 357; *Clefs de Mallarmé,* p. 146.

12 Chassé suggests giving the words their etymological meanings (âme = breath; "résumer" = take up again) and sees here a description of the smoker trying to blow his smoke rings toward the ceiling. This tempting explanation in no way excludes the other. Once again, Mallarmé has played on the several meanings of each word.

were positioned along twenty pages like somber constellations
in a pale sky. A variety of type faces: roman, italics, capitals
and lower case, seemed joined through some mysterious alchemy. Sometimes a single word appeared on a white page,
sometimes the lines rushed on, crowded and disorderly, as
if dragged along by a tornado. The sentences seemed to be
without continuity, like the incoherent monologue of a mad-
man.

Indeed, on March 30, while showing Paul Valéry the galley
proofs of his latest poem, "Un Coup de Dés jamais n'abolira
le Hasard" (A Throw of the Dice will never abolish Chance),
Mallarmé said to him, "Don't you find it a demented act?" In
truth, his most fervent disciples were silenced by this enigmatic
text, which has no equivalent in any of the world's literatures.
His contemporaries were not sure whether they were in the
presence of a work of genius or of an immense failure, one which
the title seemed to admit. This tragic declaration of impotency,
apparently confirmed by the obsessive image of the shipwreck,
seemed to be the response, thirty years later, to Igitur's out-
rageous ambition to fix the infinite and recreate the world in a
throw of the dice. No one near the poet dared say too much
about it, and after his death the critics preferred not to men-
tion it. Thibaudet was the first, in 1913, to attempt an analysis.
He noted that it was constructed around the theme of a failure.
Since then, the commentators have more or less followed
Thibaudet's general interpretation. We shall not break with
what has become the classical interpretation in our endeavor
to situate the poem in Mallarmé's work and the Symbolist
movement.

Very recently, "Un Coup de Dés" has been the object of
renewed attention and interpretations. Claude Roulet and, with
infinitely more rigor, Robert Green Cohn have both attempted
a minute and methodical exegesis. It is still too early to judge
the exact value of their efforts. Claude Roulet seems, unfortunately, to have developed his interpretation from an a priori
idea which is badly adapted to what is known about Mallarmé's
thought. Cohn's ingenious, extremely penetrating comments
must also be sifted, despite their attractiveness. The years to
come will undoubtedly see new investigations of the poem. As

of today, it can be said that the traditional interpretation of "Un Coup de Dés" must be entirely revised.

One point seems established. The "Coup de Dés" has nothing to do with any fantasy or isolated experience in Mallarmé's poetic career. It is the culmination of an entire lifetime of effort and research, more particularly of those "ten years of thought" which in 1886 Mallarmé deemed indispensable for anyone who wished to be a poet worthy of the name. Although it does not constitute the Great Work—and Mallarmé had already recognized in 1885, in his Autobiography, that he knew not who could achieve such a Work—it is uncontestably a "completed fragment," as several bits of evidence prove. First, there is a note of Mallarmé's in which he offers Gide "this first attempt, this groping." Then there is Gustave Kahn's declaration in *Symbolistes et Décadents* (Symbolists and Decadents), in which he speaks of nine other similar poems which were to follow "Un Coup de Dés"; and Claudel's statement, based on personal conversations with the poet, that "In Mallarmé's mind, this work was only the first essay of a great poem which was to contain the explanation of the world" (*Positions et Propositions* [Positions and Propositions]).

The "Coup de Dés" is clearly, then, a fragment of the Book glimpsed in the manuscript notes published by Scherer. We are not only invited, but required, to seek in it the "orphic explanation of the Earth" of which Mallarmé had spoken to Verlaine and to decipher the "equations" of Mallarmé's dream in "the very rhythm of the Book, impersonal and living even in its pagination." Finally, it represents the application of the new principles proclaimed in many a page of *Divagations* and reaffirmed in the preface Mallarmé gave his poem when it appeared in *Cosmopolis*. Let us review the essential points of these new views with emphasis on what they demand of the reader:

1. Mallarmé starts with an observation: A short poem is always surrounded by a great deal of blank space. A better use of this white, which is like silence arranged around the work, is to *disperse* it over the page according to the requirements of the thought or the meaning.

2. As a result, poetry will become an art of time. The reader will be constrained "now to accelerate, now to slow up the

movement" according to the disposition of the sentences. It
will also be an art of space, in which the page settings take on
new importance. They will become a figuration of thought and
somehow present "an exact spiritual setting" in the theatrical
sense, the poetic work becoming a reduction of the play. In the
presence of such a work, the reader must be attentive to the
placement and the *face* of the text. As Mallarmé wrote to Gide,
one can sometimes see in it "a vessel listing from the top of one
page to the bottom of another," sometimes a constellation really
taking on "the look of a constellation."

3. The unity in such a placement of words is no longer the
line. Moreover, it is difficult to see whether this "poem" is in
verse or prose. It is the culmination, a synthesis of the two. More
precisely, the "attempt participates unexpectedly in the particular pursuits dear to our time: free verse and the prose poem."
This synthesis finally substitutes a new unity for the line of
verse: the page, or rather, the double-page spread, which assures
"simultaneous viewing" by its typographical arrangement. Each
such viewing, while connected to the others, will have its own
meaning and power of suggestion, related to its figurative, repre-
sentational value. Within each viewing the words and lines will
appear as "so many prismatic subdivisions of the Idea." One
finds here again that image so dear to Mallarmé: the mutual
and trailing flames of precious stones.

4. The poet is not content with playing with page makeup;
he also plays with type faces, which give more or less importance to each idea by their form or significance. What he thus
obtains is no longer a simple literary text, but a *musical score*,
in which "the difference in type face between the preponderant,
secondary, and subsidiary motifs dictates their importance for
an oral reading. The placement at the top, bottom, or middle of
the page notes whether to raise or lower the intonation." This
is perhaps a discreet recollection of the "Démon de l'Analogie"
and the falling intonation "susceptible to condolences" with
which Mallarmé pronounced, "The Penultimate is dead." In
any case, it invites us to hear and mime the text within ourselves as much as to read it, and to be able to decipher the
"syntax of a thought" amidst the interwoven sentences and
letters. Even grammar, as he remarked in an 1895 fragment,

is "a latent and particular philosophy as well as the skeleton of the language." Is he not treating a subject of "pure and complex imagination or intellect" in the form of a symphony?

It would be impossible to discuss or summarize in a few pages the principal interpretations proposed for "Un Coup de Dés," much less propose a new one. After these preliminary remarks, we can only trace several means of access while showing how the problem of interpretation has been renewed by recent investigation, notably R. G. Cohn's. His chief merit has been to dispute those who had claimed that the work has merely a single, linear meaning, when Mallarmé had clearly intended to give it many superimposed meanings, after the fashion of the cosmos itself.

The reader must pay very close attention. He is first struck by what Mallarmé made most visible, the choice of type faces. Most noticeable is the "preponderant motif" which runs along the work in capital letters: **"UN COUP DE DÉS / JAMAIS / N'ABOLIRA / LE HASARD"** (A THROW OF THE DICE / NEVER / WILL ABOLISH / CHANCE). The four parts of this motif occur at four different parts of the poem. They appear at various heights on the page: approximately in the middle, three-quarters of the way down, at the bottom, and then again three-quarters of the way down, in an undulating movement. With reference to the sentence in "la Musique et les Lettres" on the "symphonic equation of the seasons," Cohn feels that this undulating movement could very well suggest that of time. On the plane of a cyclical movement, the four phases would represent the four seasons, or the traditional "four ages." This situates the movement in a cosmogonic perspective.

The famous sentence was for a long time regarded as a confession of defeat: an unarguable expression of the impotency of man and of his Act, whatever it might be, before the blind forces of the Cosmos. But such an admission would strangely contradict the profound intention of the poem as well as all of Mallarmé's declarations on "chance vanquished word by word." Would so many years of meditation and effort really have culminated in this banal statement? Some have sought a less simplistic interpretation for the formula. In its etymological

meaning, the word "hasard" (chance) is "a throw of six in a
game of dice" (Gengoux). Cohn thus found a second, tautologi-
cal meaning of the sentence, which is approximately this: "A
throw of the dice will never abolish a throw of the dice." This
pun of sorts expresses the notion that the world is an eternal
recommencement, subject to an immense cyclic rhythm, the
development of the initial paradox according to which "the
actual implies the potential." In accordance with Mallarmé's
most constant ideas, especially those of "Igitur," Chance would
be more precisely *what is included in Nothingness*, in a state
of equilibrium between all opposites, i.e., in infinite Possibility.
The key line of the poem returns to formulate, in the manner
of an inexorable, objective statement, the fundamental cosmic
law which decrees that no thought, no creation, no *unique*
combination (conferring on the first words "un coup de dés" all
their polyvalent and symbolic value) can exhaust or even
modify infinite Possibility.

The "secondary motif" and the "subsidiary motifs" are de-
ployed around this key sentence and its broad, fundamental,
wavelike movement. The secondary motif unfolds from the
word "JAMAIS." In smaller capitals, it develops the unique,
eternal aspect of the envisaged act: "QUAND BIEN MÊME
LANCÉ DANS DES CIRCONSTANCES ÉTERNELLES
DU FOND D'UN NAUFRAGE" (even when launched into
eternal circumstances from the depths of a shipwreck). It also
introduces a human presence into this immense cosmic framework: "SOIT . . . LE MAÎTRE" (whether . . . the Master).
The word "MAÎTRE" must be read in its fullest, richest sense:
not only the pilot of a ship, the Captain, a poet, Mallarmé,
but every man, Man, the always-dreamed-of hero for whom
Hamlet had always been Mallarmé's symbol. The general meaning of the poem actually emerges from the secondary motif and
its insertion into the preponderant motif. It is very precisely
the "unique subject" that Mallarmé had formulated in his
article on *Hamlet* in 1886: "For, know this well, there is no
other subject: the *antagonism* in man between the dream and
the fatalities of his existence administered by misfortune."

We can begin to grasp the internal wealth of the poem only
if we follow page by page, as one follows the multiple move-

ments of the waves on the moving surface of the sea, the diverse subsidiary motifs, their placement, detours, and arabesques; and by deciphering the many possible meanings of each group of words and each image.

After the initial shock, "UN COUP DE DÉS," which suggests the original "one," the very act of Creation, and then its projection into time—a somewhat eternal time with no particular limitations—one notices on the third double page the "original abyss," the Chaos in which everything is confused. Bleached by the foam, breaking forth in an effort at vertical aspiration, it is transformed into a hollow, a gaping depth in which everything is summed up. At the same time, it becomes the hull of a ship pitching and listing. Its jibsail evokes a wing —dream or poetry—impotent to fly or leap.

Then, on Page 4,[13] the forces of life and of chance are unfurled in the tempest. The Master has surged forth one day in its midst—Man, the primitive and ancestral Hero. He opposes thought to nothingness, confronts destiny with his will, hurling the "unique Number which can be no other" at the storm, trying to bring the many back to the one and make chance necessity. But he has hesitated. So, engulfed by the waves, he gives way to his son, "puerile shadow," Igitur and Hamlet, the ambiguous offspring of an ancestor's will and the blind chance of the waves. Here the question is more one of betrothal than of marriage, of the idle chance that will make him a phantom of deeds, lurching between contraries, hesitating before the absurdity of every act, but determined in his folly to brave the absurd.

Page 5: The intervention of human presence and thought is drawn in italics (suggesting both a more subtle and more important event). This simple insinuation will mysteriously unwind the spirals of poetry and dream around silence and the virgin abyss: "COMME SI" (as if). . . . As if something really were going to happen, an internal drama symbolized by the solitary feather lost in the middle of the next page (Page 6). A feather: wing? foam?—Hamlet's feather, both the ornament of midnight's cap (and so presented in the graphics of

13 As is customary in recent Mallarmé criticism, Page with a capital letter designates the full double page of "Un Coup de Dés."

the page), instrument of art, and messenger of the ideal. This "bitter prince of the reefs" who is also Everyman, Mallarmé, the poet, modern man, the "Type without a previous name," coifs himself with it as if with an heroic mark of a reason that wants at least "to contain" a destiny that he cannot resist— as if with lightning, ready to strike or flash in silence, in the night.[14]

"*SI*" (Page 8) is the perceptible note of the whole poem and the point of departure for a new and essential subsidiary motif: "*SI / C'ÉTAIT / LE NOMBRE / CE SERAIT*" (if it were the number it would be). It joins the principal motif and falls upon "**LE HASARD.**" The "*SI*" introduces the supreme hyperbole of art, the scintillating crest of vertigo (like St. Elmo's fire glittering at the top of a mast). It brings forth an ephemeral vision of the dream, a "faux manoir tout de suite évaporé en brumes" (false manor immediately dissolving in fog) as in Poe's "Fall of the House of Usher," a tomblike rock; a summing up of the Work with which the poet had claimed to impose a limit on the infinite.

This work, a true constellation, "issu stellaire" (cosmic issue), is thrown like dice on the right side of Page 9 as the unique *NUMBER*, the sole authentic witness to an existence, to a beginning and an end, a figured multiplicity which terminates in an illumination of evidence. Nevertheless, this Work will finally be reabsorbed in the undifferentiated great All, in the fusion of opposites, in **CHANCE.** Once the apocalyptic shipwreck is accomplished, the feather will in fact fall into the abyss of origins to be buried where everything assumes an identical neutrality. Then, according to the subsidiary, or rather

14 A passage from "Solennité" marvelously clarifies this page of "Un Coup de Dés": "What a spectacle! The world is contained in it. If it provokes some august idea, a book in our hand supplants all theater, not by reducing theater to oblivion but, on the contrary, by mysteriously recalling its function. The metaphysical sky propagated by the lightning of verse, that most excellent artifice for simulating and gradually incarnating heroes (in exactly as much as one must perceive in order to avoid being uncomfortable with them, a brushstroke); this spiritually and magnificently illuminated depth of ecstasy is the purest of ourselves, carried by us always, ready to flash out at the opportunity which, in existence or outside of art, is always lacking" (*Oeuvres complètes*, p. 334).

complementary, motif on Page 10, "RIEN / N'AURA EU LIEU / QUE LE LIEU" (nothing will have taken place but the place), the cycle closes. Everything returns ineluctably to the primordial ocean, an abstract and empty place disturbed only by an "inférieur clapotis quelconque" (some sort of inferior splashing), a pure horizon where all reality dissolves.

At least on the human plane; for on the last double Page, in a sort of coda to the poem, the complementary motif unexpectedly jumps back again: "EXCEPTÉ / PEUT-ÊTRE / UNE CONSTELLATION" (except perhaps a constellation), flung down on the white page like a new, mysterious throw of the dice. But if something is going to take place it will be "à l'altitude" (in altitude), beyond the human and even the cosmic plane: "aussi loin qu'un endroit fusionne avec au delà" (as far away as to make a place fuse with the beyond). It would be somewhere on a metaphysical level, "sur quelque surface vacante et supérieure" (on some vacant and superior surface), where all distinctions are abolished, but the Spirit's lines of force converge and combine "selon telle obliquité par telle déclivité de feux" (according to angles caused by the slope of the fires). This something would be what the "Sonnet in *-yx*" had indicated: a mysterious CONSTELLATION, the seven stars of the Big Dipper which summarize the ultimate reality, the Spirit. The constellation is "froide d'oubli et de désuétude" (cold with oblivion and disuse) because it is beyond any individual consciousness or human memory. Yet it contains within itself the supreme game, the total tally of the Spirit, including all the becoming of this Spirit, in turn watching, doubting, rolling, shining, and meditating before ending at total fixity, stopped by "quelque point dernier qui le sacre" (some last point which consecrates it). That is the metaphysical Septentrion, both the point of origin and the terminus of all things. So the Poem finally closes, like Creation itself, not on the cosmic plane of the preceding Page, but on the metaphysical plane, with this formula: "Toute Pensée émet un Coup de Dés" (Every Thought emits a Throw of the Dice). The indisputable primacy of the Spirit and its powers is serenely **asserted.**

André Gide called "Un Coup de Dés" "the most extreme point to which the human spirit has ventured." Certain experiences, such as those of the great mystics, perhaps led further into the domain of spirituality in another way. But on the poetic level Mallarmé's adventure is certainly unique. His attempt to give poetry the dimensions of cosmogony through typography and word suggestion was more daring than any poetic endeavor up to the twentieth century. The esthetic quality of the poem can be judged more diversely. I tend to think, together with R. G. Cohn, that only a long intimacy with Mallarmé's poetry, as well as with this unprecedented piece, allows one to make judgments in good faith. Frequent rereading would probably lead one little by little to become sensitive to its internal reflections, its transparencies, and the radiation of its many flames, to its richly complex musical structure, just as an orchestra conductor, by dint of rereading the score of a symphony, finally hears the interplay of all the instruments in his inner ear. Then, instead of seeming to be a constellation cold with boredom and disuse, the "Coup de Dés" would perhaps become, at least for some, the starkest expression of that human anguish that sometimes strikes us to the core in the face of human insignificance, an anguish that only a renunciation of all egotism can transform into serenity.

In 1897 Mallarmé said one day to a friend, "Writing a book today is making a will." He was no doubt thinking particularly of the "Coup de Dés," but he certainly felt that this was only a part of his testament. All the rest, those key pieces in the long-meditated work, were still in his head or in scattered notes. He may have hoped that the calm of Valvins would permit him to sketch out, if not finish, the poetic cathedral in which he wanted to concentrate all the sounds of the world, so that their deafening echoes would reverberate as far as infinity.

But fate did not indulge him with the laborious, fertile retirement that he had awaited and hoped for all his life long. On September 8, 1898, while working on some new poem, he was suddenly overcome by an attack of shortness of breath. Abruptly confronted by death, and thinking only of the women whom he was going to leave behind him with meager resources, he scratched a few shaky lines which are a sort of testament in reverse:

You will not be surprised that I am thinking of the half-century pile of my notes which will only be a great nuisance to you: do not expect one sheet to be of any service. Only I could draw from them what is there... I would have done it, had I not been cheated of the last years I so needed. Consequently, burn: there is no literary heritage there, my poor children... And you, the only beings in the world capable of respecting to that extent an entire lifetime of sincere devotion to art, believe that it would have been very beautiful.

The next morning, a new spasm carried him away.

By Way of Conclusion

IT IS somehow unfitting to draw conclusions from an adventure such as Mallarmé's. Who can claim to have traveled far enough along the ways of meditation and poetic experience to be capable of measuring the true value of his life and work? And now that they are the object of renewed attention, who can foresee the wealth and significance that may be discovered in them tomorrow? At present, one can only propose several provisional judgments.

First of all, can one speak of *failure* in Mallarmé's work? We know now that the Book was to have been a synthesis of every genre: theater, dance, and even music. It would have presented "the sum of the relationships existing among all things" through an ingenious system of movable pages and permutations. What he achieved in poetry has no common measure with the ideal of his dreams. But he knew better than anyone that incommensurability is part of man's nature; he confided one day to Camille Mauclair,

> But we are all failures, Mauclair! How can we be otherwise, when we measure our finiteness against infinity? We place our short life and feeble strength in the balance with an ideal which, by definition, cannot be attained. We are predestined failures. . . . From that point of view, I think I am more entitled to the epithet than anyone.

The question is not so much whether he realized his ideal, but whether his real work was or was not in rapport with what he had planned to write. The more one penetrates his true

intentions and the meaning of his work, the more one is convinced that he did really create, if not the Work he had
dreamed of, at least, as he wished, "one completed fragment."
This opinion is confirmed by the manuscript notebook of the
"Book" and can only be reinforced by exegeses yet to come.

His intentions were on such a level that their value can be
judged only in terms of one's own convictions. If we agree that
every human drama ends in shipwreck and that our lot on
earth is to fence with shadows, can we reproach Mallarmé for
having at least elevated this shipwreck to an eminent dignity by
situating it *sub specie aeternitatis*, or, as he said, "in eternal
circumstances"? There can be no discussion of Mallarmé's
failure, then, but only of the failure of man as seen by Mallarmé. The hero of Mallarmé's drama is merely man in all
his individuality, a particular consciousness. If this man can
become "impersonal," if he can bypass contingency and difference to identify with All-Nothingness, drama and shipwreck are then inscribed in the natural course of things. They
are just so many accidents which occur in the cycle of cosmic
manifestation and are finally negligible if considered from
the heights of "some vacant, superior surface," i.e., from the
absolute Spirit. Mallarmé's conception of poetry thus joins
the oriental and notably the Hindu concepts, by which poetry,
like any art, should be an explanation and reproduction of
the Great Play of universal manifestation. The notion is essentially mystical because it makes poetry tend toward silence,
as manifestation itself tends toward its own reabsorption in
the unmanifest.

In contrast is the Judeo-Christian tradition for which creation
has meaning, direction, and finality; to end not in a reabsorption
but in the most total and perfect manifestation of divine glory.
This finality makes poetry an instrument of the manifestation,
and the poet is, as Claudel put it, "fondé de pouvoirs de Dieu"
(God's holding agent). This tradition does not postulate the
final failure of all efforts. On the contrary, it maintains the
ambiguity of failure and victory, even to the last act, and vali-
dates the poetic act at the same time. The poetic act is given its
part of responsibility in this adventure and is viewed as a manifestation of the Word, rather than as a preparation for silence.

Mallarmé's attempt must always be at least relatively a failure
in the mind of a Claudel, not on the level of realization, but
on the level of *intent*, to the extent that this intent is bound to
what might be called a metaphysics of failure. For Claudel,
Mallarmé was above all else an excellent teacher of attention,
whose admirable lesson was how to read in the world's book
and constantly ask, "What does that mean?" but in whose eyes
the key to this book, once found, would have been of no use.

Metaphysical controversy aside, the two concepts are not so
contradictory on a poetic plane as they might seem. Whatever
his convictions, the poet always uses the same material, language; and he does not use it as laymen do. Classic or Romantic, Impressionist or partisan of Art for Art's Sake, idealist or
even realist, through poetry he expresses what daily language
does not convey. It is not the least of Mallarmé's merits to have
so formally distinguished poetic language from this other instrument of "universal reporting." He was not formulating a
personal theory or a doctrine for a school when he pointed out
that daily language is content to translate concepts or designate
objects, while poetic language attempts to give words their
metaphorical value, i.e., their power of many meanings; essentially, its role is to suggest. He was elucidating the very concept
of poetry as it had been incorporated in the works of the great
poets of all times. The term "symbol," which he seems to have
demonstrated as important to the literary movement that grew
out of him, characterizes this value of inherent multiple meaning. Each poet now has his own manner of envisioning the
symbol, according to his own philosophy. Mallarmé sees it as a
means of climbing up from the world of material objects to
the mystical or metaphysical world of pure concepts. Verlaine
sees it, more simply, as the fleeting reality of states of mind.
Rimbaud attempts to restore magical powers to it so as to
bring forth a truer, richer, more harmonious, concrete reality.
These are all aspects of the symbol, but they do not detract
from its principal function, which is to restore to language its
original power and mystery.

And this is Mallarmé's other great merit: for the first time
in our era, he totally and *consciously* (rather than instinctively,

like other poets) willed and assumed the mystery of poetic
language. Once again, his hermeticism was neither a desire to
mystify nor a puerile quest for a new poetics at any price. It
was the result of an effort, constantly pursued during an entire
lifetime, to purge poetry of all foreign elements, *to bring it
back to its essence.* Such intransigence brings with it certain
risks, not the least of which is to alienate those who turn to
poetry for escape or facile enjoyment. But one cannot in good
faith refuse to recognize the legitimacy of this approach, any
more than one can refuse to acknowledge Mallarmé's concern
for efficacity and, indeed, his real efficacy itself.

Criticism long considered his work a mandarin's game. But
for several years now, having reread *Divagations* with more
care, the critics have noticed that the hermit of Valvins and
the talker of the rue de Rome was less withdrawn from life
than he had wanted, or seemed to affect, to be. Now attention
is paid to his preoccupation with the magical powers of
language: "I say that a secret parity exists between the old
practices [of witchcraft] and the sorcery that is and will be
poetry" ("Magie" [Magic]). Emphasis is placed on his concern
with having an effect on the crowd, and finding the ideal
formula to restore to art, and more especially to poetry, a
ceremonial and sacred ritual such as still exists in the Catholic
Church and to a certain extent in music:

> Here recognize henceforth in drama, the Passion, to broaden the
> canonical acceptance or, as it was the ceremonious esthetic of the
> Church, with the fiery pinwheel of hymns, an assimilation of man
> to the tetralogy of the Year ("Catholicisme" [Catholicism]).

He had, moreover, dreamed of giving readings during which
he would have commented on the meaning of his Book for a
few chosen listeners in a carefully regulated ceremony.

Some critics even bow to a currently fashionable terminology
and speak of Mallarmé's "engagement" (commitment). This
is actually not too farfetched. Every authentic poet commits
his lifetime to the act of writing. No one considers this act the
sole justification of his life more than did Mallarmé.

His commitment was no mere intent. Undeniably, Mallarmé
taught a lesson not only to a few direct disciples, but, in a

much more diffused manner, to all the poetry and even all the literature of the first half of the twentieth century. His endeavor was in one sense an "impasse," as he declared one day to Le Cardonnel. Among those of his disciples who wished to follow the same path, only Valéry, a half-century later, attained any prominence. Even he retained from the Master only his poetic ambition, discarding the metaphysical ambition, which seemed to him a vain illusion. But Mallarmé's effect reached much further than his circle of initiates. His influence was directly exerted in many foreign countries, beginning with Germany and Stefan George. More important, the intransigent quality of his endeavor obtained the more or less official recognition, as legitimate and necessary, of obscurity in poetry. He had liberated the poetic instrument once and for all from the harness of three centuries of rationalistic French rhetoric, up to and including Romanticism. He had forcefully established that the function of the poet, and of the writer in general, is to decipher the mystery of the world, which carries its own explanation with it. Jean Royère's neo-Mallarmism and the pseudo-Mallarmism of more or less ponderous imitators matter little after this. Mallarmé's greatness depends less on the number of his successors than on the expansion and vitality of his work itself. After a half-century, it provides more sustenance than ever for the reflections of poets and critics in every land.

Bibliographical Note

IT IS to be noted that the understanding of Mallarmé has been largely revised since 1940 by the discovery of the correspondence and of new manuscripts, the latter presenting hitherto-unknown early versions of numerous poems. Thus, for the period before that date I shall list below only those works that are in any case the basis of the study of Mallarmé. Emphasis will be placed on works of recent date.

I. EDITIONS AND BIBLIOGRAPHY

Mallarmé, Stéphane. *Oeuvres complètes*, Henri Mondor and G. Jean-Aubry, eds. Paris, Gallimard, Bibliothèque de la Pléiade, 1945. This critical edition, which gives, in addition to an important bibliography, all the variants in the manuscripts known to date, replaces all preceding, partial editions. Until the publication of the complete *Correspondence*, copious extracts can be found in Henri Mondor's *Vie de Mallarmé* (see below), as well as in

———. *Propos sur la poésie*, Henri Mondor, ed. Monaco, Éditions du Rocher, 1946. These may be rounded out by reference to the *Correspondance inédite entre Mallarmé et Henri Roujon* (Geneva, Cailler, 1949) and *L'Amitié entre Mallarmé et Rodenbach* (Geneva, Cailler, 1949).

Monda, Maurice and François Montel. *Bibliographie des poètes maudits*; Vol. I, *Stéphane Mallarmé*. Paris, Giraud-Badin, 1927. 2 vols.

II. BIOGRAPHY

Mondor, Henri. *Vie de Mallarmé.* Paris, Gallimard, 1941. A very important work, which completely altered knowledge of Mallarmé's life. Also:

Faure, Gabriel. *Mallarmé à Tournon.* Paris, Horiz. de France, 1946.

Mondor, Henri. *Histoire d'un Faune.* Paris, Gallimard, 1948.

————. *Eugène Lefébure, sa vie, ses lettres à Mallarmé.* Paris, Gallimard, 1951.

————. *Mallarmé plus intime.* Paris, Gallimard, 1944.

III. GENERAL STUDIES

Bo, Carlo. *Mallarmé.* Milona, Rosa and Boillo, 1945.

Dujardin, Édouard. *Mallarmé par un des siens.* Paris, Messein. 1936.

Goffin, Robert. *Mallarmé vivant.* Paris, Nizet, 1956.

Mauclair, Camille. *Mallarmé chez lui.* Paris, Grasset, 1935.

Mauron, Charles. *Introduction à la psychanalyse de Mallarmé.* Neuchâtel, la Baconnière, 1950.

————. *Mallarmé l'obscur.* Paris, Denoël, 1941.

Michaud, Guy. *Message poétique du Symbolisme, La Doctrine symboliste (passim).* Paris, Nizet, 1947. 4 vols.

Miomandre, Francis de. *Mallarmé.* Lausanne, Bader-Dufour, 1948.

Orliac, Antoine. *Mallarmé tel qu'en lui-même.* Paris, Mercure de France, 1948.

Wais, Kurt. *Mallarmé, Dichtung, Weisheit, Haltung.* Munich, C. H. Beck'sche Verlag, 1952 (new edition, entirely revised).

Les Lettres, special number devoted to Mallarmé, Paris, 1948.

Le Point, special number, Lanzac, 1944.

Stéphane Mallarmé, essais et témoignages. Neuchâtel, 1942.

IV. STUDIES OF MALLARMÉ'S POETRY AND ESTHETICS

Aish, Deborah. *La métaphore dans l'oeuvre de Mallarmé.* Paris, Droz, 1938.

Beausire, Pierre. *Mallarmé, poésie et poétique.* Lausanne, Mermod, 1949.

Chassé, Charles. *Les Clefs de Mallarmé*. Paris, Aubier, 1954.

――――. *Lueurs sur Mallarmé*. Paris, N. R. C., 1947.

Cohn, Robert Green. *Un coup de dés jamais n'abolira le hasard*. Paris, Les Lettres, 1952.

Davies, Gardner. *Les "tombeaux" de Mallarmé, essai d'exégèse raisonnée*. Paris, Corti, 1950.

Delfel, Guy. *L'esthétique de S. Mallarmé*. Paris, Flammarion, 1951.

Fiser, E. *Le symbole littéraire chez Wagner, Baudelaire, Mallarmé, Bergson et Proust*. Paris, Corti, 1942.

Gengoux, Jacques. *Le symbolisme de Mallarmé*. Paris, Nizet, 1950.

Noulet, Émilie. *Dix poèmes de S. Mallarmé*. Geneva, Droz, 1948.

――――. *L'oeuvre poétique de Stéphane Mallarmé*. Paris, Droz, 1940.

――――. *Suite mallarméenne*. Paris, Maison du Livre français, 1959.

Poulet, Georges. *Espace et temps mallarméens*. Neuchâtel, la Baconnière, 1951.

Roulet, Claude. *Éléments de poétique mallarméenne d'après le poème: Un coup de dés jamais n'abolira le hasard*. Neuchâtel, Éditions du Griffon, 1947.

Schérer, Jacques. *L'expression littéraire dans l'oeuvre de Mallarmé*. Paris, Droz, 1947.

――――. *Le "Livre" de Mallarmé*. Paris, Gallimard, 1957.

Soula, Camille. *Gloses sur Mallarmé*. Paris, Éd., Diderot, 1945.

Thibaudet, Albert. *La poésie de S. Mallarmé*. Gallimard, 1913.

V. ENGLISH TRANSLATIONS

Mallarmé, Stéphane. *Poems*, tr. Roger Fry with commentaries by Charles Mauron. Binghamton (N.Y.), New Directions, 1951.

――――. *Selected Poems*, tr. C. F. MacIntyre. Berkeley, University of California Press, 1959.

VI STUDIES IN ENGLISH

Bowra, C. M. *The Heritage of Symbolism*. London, Macmillan, 1943.

Chisholm, A. R. *Towards Herodiade: A Literary Genealogy.* Melbourne University Press, 1934.

Cohn, Robert Green. *Mallarmé's "Un Coup de Dés."* New Haven, Yale French Studies, 1949.

Cooperman, Hayse. *The Aesthetics of Mallarmé.* New York, The Koffern Press, 1933.

Davies, Gardner. *Stéphane Mallarmé: Fifty Years of Research.* Oxford, Blackwell, French Studies, January 1947.

Ellis, Arthur. *Stéphane Mallarmé in English Verse.* London, Cape, 1927.

Fowlie, Wallace. *Mallarmé.* University of Chicago Press, 1953.

——. *Mallarmé as Hamlet: A Study of "Igitur."* Yonkers (N.Y.), Alicat Bookshop Press, 1949.

Lowell, Amy. *Six French Poets.* New York, Macmillan, 1916.

Mauron, Charles. *Introduction to the Psychoanalysis of Mallarmé,* tr. Archibald Henderson, Jr. and Will McLencon. Berkeley, University of California Press, 1963.

Symons, Arthur. *The Symbolist Movement in Literature.* London, Heinemann, 1899.

Wilson, Edmund. *Axel's Castle.* New York, Scribner, 1931.

Woolley, Grange. *Stéphane Mallarmé.* Madison (N.J.), Drew University, 1942.